THE SOUND OF SILENCE

Other books by Graham Clews

Jessica Jones and the Gates of Penseron (2006)

Eboracum, The Village (2007)

Eboracum, The Fortress (2008)

Eboracum, Carved in Stone (2010)

Politically Detained (2015)

A Slightly Tainted Hero (2015)

THE SOUND OF
SILENCE

Graham Clews

THE SOUND OF SILENCE

Copyright © 2015, Graham Clews.

All rights reserved. No part of this publication may be reproduced, stored in a retrieval system, or transmitted in any form or by any means, electronic, mechanical, photocopying, recording, or otherwise, without written permission of the author and publisher.

Published by Rubicon Developments, Westlock, Canada

ISBN 978-1-988048-21-5

Publication assistance and
digital printing in Canada by

www.pagemaster.ca

The book has no dedication.
It is written with the sincere hope that any reader
who has experienced this sort of thing will find
something of value inside.

Prologue

Life's significant events, particularly the nasty ones, often return from the past, haunting one's conscience like dark, yet sedulous, ghosts. They are the unsought phantoms of lost conflicts between right and wrong that were buried so long ago they were assumed to be dead and gone. They appear from nowhere, unexpectedly resurrecting a culpable conscience that was thought to have been interred with the corpse of the same specter. Alas, ghosts such as these will never completely go away. But then, why should they? When a person ignores shameful events that should never have been ignored; when one fails to do what is right, either through ignorance or convenience; when someone does not stop to ponder on what might happen to others rather than just themselves; then they must live with the consequences. Age will never ease the guilt that rises from one's past misjudgments. Age does, in fact, exacerbate it.

My father's phone call was such a significant event, the final act in a tragedy that should have ended three decades before. The call took place one evening in the autumn of nineteen eighty seven. It began with a minute or two of the usual preamble—how are you, and what have you been doing, all that sort of thing—and then he got down to the real reason for the call. There had to be a real reason. He rarely called otherwise. This time it was to tell me that he had been arrested. There was no need to ask why. My father was a pedophile, and I knew that. I had simply chosen to believe that he had stopped being one many years before when he assured me and everyone else, including his divorce lawyer, that he had indeed stopped, and there had been no subsequent overt evidence to contradict his word.

The real purpose of the phone call was to ask if I would advance funds in order for him to hire a defence lawyer. The line fell silent for a minute or so as I pondered the question, figuring what to say. Yet there could only be a single response. I told my father I would loan him the funds on the condition that he pled guilty. There was also no need to ask if he was.

He replied that he'd think it over, and he'd call me back. He never did. That was the last time I spoke to my father. He died just over two decades later in January of 2009, at the age of ninety one. At the time of the call, he would have been approximately the same age as I am today.

***

Once off the phone, my mind raced and not necessarily with the noblest of thoughts. The first was that 'the problem' was finally out in the open, and what did that mean to me and my family? This was selfish, of course, but after more than thirty years since first becoming a victim of father's sexual predilections, many of the old fears still remained, such as the publicity, the gossip, and the shame. Those were instinctive, but all the other fears that had once terrified a thirteen old child had long since disappeared: the effect of father's exposure on my mother and her situation, the embarrassing reaction of school friends, the threat to the security of our family's everyday living, and even the breakup of the family itself. By the time of father's phone call the latter had long since taken place, and the rest of it no longer mattered. And, as I gave it a bit more thought, neither did anything else. The imagined publicity, the gossip and the public shame, if they existed at all, they were not my problem. Nor had they ever been. They were my father's. Yet even so...

Over a quarter century has passed since the phone call and my father's crimes proved to be far more blatant than I had ever been aware, all of which came out during prosecution of the court case. Soon, other considerations began to haunt my mind. A new sense of shame began to take hold and with it a growing sense of guilt, two feelings that have intensified as the years pass by. Age has brought with it a renewed focus on those two regrettable lists that lengthen during one's lifetime: *the things we should not have done, and the things we should have done.* Each forever competes with the other in length, but in this instance the shame and the guilt could be readily found on either list.

-*I should never have kept my mouth shut about my father's sexual abuse.*

-*I should have told someone, anyone, but particularly the authorities.*

Instead, I remained silent, and others were hurt because of this. In this alone can be found perhaps the only reason that any shame and guilt need ever be felt by the sexually abused victim. It will echo through that victim's mind, slowly growing louder as he or she grows older, and it will be there until the day they die. It might well be called *The Sound of Silence*.

Chapter One

On moving to Canada...

We were typical of the immigrants arriving in Edmonton in those glorious days of the mid-fifties: European ancestry, father a World War II veteran with a trade, a stay-at-home mum, and four kids—two boys and two girls. We could have auditioned for a sitcom. I was the oldest at thirteen, the only non-Boomer. The other three were spaced out in precise, four-year increments that were more accident than design: Margaret, Angela, and the youngest, Steve, who was two and a half months short of his first birthday at the time of the move. Arriving in Canada was, and probably will always be, the greatest adventure of our lives.

Until I sat down to write this manuscript, I had always thought the reason for our emigration from England was straightforward. When we are young, we tend to believe all that adults tell us, particularly when it comes from our parents—and even the inevitable truth about Santa Claus and the Easter Bunny never gave us reason to doubt them.

The auto body repair shop our father had owned and operated in York, England, had failed, which apparently came as a surprise. Everyone else seemed to think the place was a gold mine, and often said as much. Mother certainly did, both before and after the bankruptcy—a financial catastrophe that is harshly dealt with in Britain. This is especially true when compared to the benign exceptions offered by Canadian bankruptcy law. In England, everything was on the table, including personal possessions and, not to be taken lightly, an individual's reputation. In adult circles, bankruptcy was considered worse than contracting a social disease, possibly because it was so public, and definitely untreatable.

As youngsters we saw nothing of this side of the process though, and the reasons for our leaving York were simply taken for granted: Dad's business had failed, whatever that meant, and we were moving. As kids we may not have understood the implications, but we took matters in our stride. I can remember no dramatic events, such as Dickensian bill collectors pounding on the door, or hard-nosed bailiffs ejecting the family onto the street. In fact, at no time did we feel as if the family had been indisposed at all, other than noting the bickering that occurred between our parents. Whatever process was involved, it was quiet and unobtrusive. Who knows, maybe it was even a midnight flit, but we kids didn't care. We were going to Canada!

The choice of Edmonton was one of those whims of fate that will chart the path of a person's life forever. In due course my father's application to emigrate was approved through Canada House in London, probably around March of 1956. However, he had to have a job waiting before we could leave England. Only one newspaper was available at Canada House, a copy of the *Edmonton Journal*. It could have been the *Winnipeg Free Press*, I suppose, and who knows where that would have led? *Going to Winnipeg!* Perhaps the gods were simply being kind.

Father found a want-ad in the *Journal* placed by an auto body repair shop on the south side of Edmonton that was called, quaintly enough, The Bump Shop. The business sought an experienced body repair man, and Father applied by mail. In the 1950s the postal system was far more efficient than it is today. In fact, by comparison to today's service (which surely includes storage fees), the delivery time was marvelous—and that was back when airplanes still used propellers. A letter took three days to arrive going westward, and four days at the most when flying east. Delivery time was as reliable as a Whitehurst clock, and so three days was all it took for the letter to reach the body shop's owner, Paul Brittain. On the fourth day Father received a phone call. He was hired sight unseen and told to get to Canada as soon as he could.

The bureaucracy was also more efficient back then, even for passports and immigration papers. The phone call came around the end of March, and by mid-April Father was on the job in this new and wondrous country called Canada. Mother arrived in late June with the four kids, following what was—for the kids, anyway—an idyllic couple of months in York, as the 1955–56 school year drew to a close.

We moved in with two of our most favourite people in the world, my maternal grandparents, whom we called Nan and Pop. For the weeks between mid-April and June 22, ninety percent of the rules were promptly tossed out the window. Not only that, the pressure of doing well at school eased dramatically, because who cared about marks anymore? An exciting journey was in our future, a voyage that for children who had hardly ventured anywhere, defied the imagination. It was a move to the Wild West of Northern America! The two kids who were old enough to understand, Margaret and I, couldn't wait to leave.

For my mother and her parents, it was doubtless the most stressful and tearful period of their lives, and likely remained so as long as they lived. We children were callously oblivious to this, including the worst of it, the final goodbye at the Southampton docks. With my father already in Canada, Pop took charge. He shepherded his daughter and his grandchildren to the south coast of England, taking us all the way from York by train (he lived to be ninety-three and never did possess a driver's licence). We abandoned him at the foot of the ship's impossibly long gangplank, but only after a boatload of hugs and tear-soaked kisses.

Just as I turned to grasp the railing and follow Mum up the sloped walkway, Pop grabbed hold of my shoulders. He bent down and hugged me tight, and with eyes brimming tears, he said, "Look after your mum for me, Graham."

I solemnly nodded and promised I would do exactly that, but to be miserably honest, at that age I had no idea what my grandfather was really, truly telling me. Nor had I a clue of how he must have felt. Such is the callow insensitivity of a thirteen-year-old. If only we could go back with the knowledge we have now, and do things over. Yet if we were able, how could we stand it?

Whenever I think of that departure, an excerpt from the biography of a British airline pilot comes to mind, a man who flew the trans-Atlantic run and whose name, unfortunately, I've long forgotten (I think it might be found in that impeccable source of all information, *Reader's Digest*). During the fifties, one of his regular flights departed from Prestwick, carrying Scottish immigrants on their way to a new life in Canada. These flights would take off late at night, from an airport noted for its miserable weather—but then, I suppose that applies to the whole of Scotland. He claimed that the saddest part of his job was watching the passengers climb aboard, each with one eye on the airplane, the other on the huddled crowd that stood waving goodbye.

The wind always seemed to be blowing hard, as it so often does off the harsh coast of Scotland. The teeming rain would gust sideways, lashing in sheets across the glistening tarmac as the families trudged the short distance to the waiting aircraft. Tears would be in everyone's eyes, especially those of the women and children, blending with the rain as they reluctantly climbed the boarding ramp. And behind them, shivering alongside the airport building in the dimly lit shadows of the night, would be the relatives, often in the hundreds, and all them singing, "Will ye no' come back again?"

My, oh my ... however ever did they cope?

The first leg of our journey was the better part of a week aboard the Cunard liner HMS *Scythia*. The second leg was *supposed* to have been a train trip that lasted three full days and would have taken us across most of Canada. This nine or ten day trek had all the ingredients of a glorious holiday—for everyone but Mother. Bear in mind that all four of us were aged thirteen and under, with one only nine months old and still in diapers (or nappies as we called them); and accommodation on both the ship and the train would prove to be a small cabin with four narrow bunks. Mother did manage to gain some pleasure from the voyage across the North Atlantic, particularly the food aboard ship, but the trip was quite hectic, especially on arrival. She was totally frazzled by the immigration process (Mum was never very good with forms and details), and the short rail trip from Quebec City to Montreal was a disaster. She finally gave up and phoned home—her new home, in Edmonton—to arrange air transport for the balance of the trip.

For the three older children, however, every step of the journey was a new and exciting adventure. One of the most surprising parts was the opulence on board the *Scythia*, which by today's cruise line standards really wasn't that great, not in third class, anyway. But we thought it was terrific. We had been raised in post-war Britain where food rationing, in one form or another, had finally vanished only two years before our move (July 4, 1954—England's unheralded independence day). The assortment of food that could be actually *ordered* aboard ship was amazing to our young minds. Not only was there a menu from which even a kid could choose, you could have all you wanted—even in third class! Up until that time, meals at home consisted of two choices, which were a tired joke around the family table: like it or lump it!

The excitement of that voyage! Before we left dockside, we seemed to have the run of the ship while the crew sorted things out. My oldest sister and I took the opportunity to explore, and we accidentally wandered into the first class dining room, where a huge table of food had been placed on display. A large roasted pig was the centrepiece, complete with the traditional apple stuffed in its mouth, glossy glazing, and long, wavy streaks of icing. The effect was positively medieval. We thought the fairy tale array of food was spread out waiting for us. We were terribly disappointed to find ourselves in a more Spartan dining room later that evening—until the waiter presented a menu and actually asked us children what we would like to order.

The ship must have arrived in Canadian waters as dawn was breaking, because we cruised down the incredibly broad Saint Lawrence in the cool sunshine of morning. The vessel went as far as Quebec City, where we finally disembarked. The harbour and its structures remain a foggy memory, for everything seemed so huge, but there was a large, airy brick building full of chatter and uniforms where I think we were processed. The ship's dock lay outside its wide doors like a broad, endless cliff, with the black-painted hull of Cunard's *HMS Scythia* nestled alongside. I remember peering down between the ship and the concrete wall and wondering what would happen if someone fell between.

Less than five minutes later, farther along by the bow, a distraught immigrant mother ran frantically toward the edge of the dock, where her son, a toddler of maybe two or three, stood placidly staring down at the water, maybe twenty feet below. To this day, I'm amazed the poor kid didn't fall over the edge as he turned and saw his mum hurtling toward him, shrieking and howling terror every step of the way.

There was a ton of confusion on the docks, and our poor mother became promptly and despairingly caught up in it. She stood helpless in the midst of the mayhem, a bundle of luggage at her feet and three kids hovering around her skirts, with the fourth in her arms. (She would have been thirty-two at the time.) There would probably have been tears in her eyes, for she had no idea what to do, and we certainly couldn't help.

Then, out of the blue, the proverbial white knight arrived, clad in rather drab-looking armour. He was tall, balding, and middle-aged, and carried a light brown trench coat over one arm of his brown tweed jacket. He strode along the dock as if he knew exactly where he was headed. He had almost certainly been a fellow passenger, likely a seasoned one, and his bearing marked him as ex-military. This stranger paused to study Mother, her brood, and the obvious problems; then he grinned and walked over to ask if she needed any help. The question was moot. Indeed she did, and Mum gratefully told him so!

The man also carried a single small suitcase and an umbrella the length of a walking stick. (The things that stick out in your mind!) Transferring both to one hand, he lifted the other and called for a porter. He then took charge of our confused family, guiding Mother by the elbow over to where we could find access to the train that left for Montreal. He inspected the tickets, made sure we were all set, smiled, and wished Mother all the best before going on his way. A Samaritan, and a darned good one, too—one of those many people over the years whose memory is planted forever in your mind so that you will always wonder: who was he, and whatever happened to him? Every one of us has our story, and I'd bet dollars to donuts that his was intriguing.

The train journey from the dock in Quebec City to Montreal took something like eighteen hours in humid, ninety degree heat to cover only 260 kilometres. The carriage was an oven-like zoo. Freight trains chugged by as we sat forever on grimy industrial railway sidings; diesel engines clashed back and forth as they reconnected with hundreds of boxcars; and when we did finally move, buildings and countryside chugged past the window at a snail's pace. I don't know what Mother said to Father when she tottered off the train in Montreal, but she seemed quite determined not to take another three days of this. Not long after, she grimly announced that we were all going on an airplane ride. I don't know how they found the money, but the next day the final leg of our journey was completed in luxury aboard a Trans-

Canada Air Lines four-engine Vicker's Viscount. (The company changed its name to Air Canada in 1965.)

How she managed the logistics I don't know, but Mum got us all to Dorval Airport and onto the plane. (Coincidentally, my wife and I wound up living in Montreal for a couple of years in the late sixties, and the commuter train at Dorval station proved to be the best way to get to work in downtown Montreal). Once we were at the airport, the rest of the journey was clear sailing—or I suppose flying is the correct word. The plane trip remains quite vivid, even though it was the second one of my life. The first had been a half-hour flight over London in a biplane with my father soon after the war, much against my mother's wishes.

The flight across Canada was an infinite step up the ladder from the London biplane. The Vicker's Viscount had half as many wings and four times as many engines, all of which whirled and roared starting a bare ten feet from the window where we sat in the first row of seats in economy. I sat spellbound as a couple thousand miles of Canada edged below at three hundred miles an hour. (A bit of trivia: soon after arriving I read that one of the starboard prop blades sheared off a Viscount's engine, killing the person sitting in the same seat. I always wondered if it was the same plane. I guess timing is everything.)

We arrived in Edmonton on yet another gloriously sunny day, to be reunited with Father. After a brief stay-over of a few days at the Brittain residence, which was near the current location of the Edmonton Eskimos football stadium, we moved to a rented duplex close to The Bump Shop on the south side of the river, probably during the first week of July.

It didn't take long for us three oldest kids to become completely wrapped up in our new lives. As for our Mother, well, selfish little devils that kids can be at that age, I don't suppose we gave much thought to the awful, wrenching emotions she must have felt at the time. And those emotions were no doubt trumped by those of her parents, Nan and Pop. Father, too, must have had certain regrets, though he never showed them as Mother did. Father's parents were a distant, elderly couple to whom we had paid mandatory visits, and we never did feel as close to them as we did to Nan and Pop. Only later, as I got older and had children of my own, did I even begin to realize their heartache at such an unalterable, unrelenting leave-taking.

***

We arrived in Edmonton on June 29, a date that, seven years later, would be my wedding day. The summer of 1956 was hot and dry, at least in memory. For a bunch of youngsters who were far too familiar with the fogs and rains of Yorkshire, it was simply an Eden by comparison. Despite the weather, however, Edmonton was at first a tremendous disappointment.

Several weeks before I left York, the geography master at the school I attended (we called our teachers masters back then) decided to show the class where "Clews" was going later that month. He rolled down a world map, which in those days was proudly smeared with large tracts of pink, and pointed to the largest blob with the tip of his cane. "Does anyone know the province in which Edmonton is located?"

Surprisingly, quite a few hands shot up, and among them of course was my own. The next two questions, however, proved more difficult: does anyone know the population of Edmonton, and the geography of the region surrounding the city? Not a hand went up, including mine, which earned the customary dark frown of disapproval. Once past those first coddled primary grades, school had never been one of my favourite places.

The geography master's name is long forgotten, but his image remains, that of an older, portly man with thinning fair hair who relied on a thick walking stick for balance. The first answer he gave also stuck in my mind, and it was correct, for I recently looked the figure up on the Net. The population of Edmonton was around 225,000 in 1956. But this thirteen-year-old kid from Yorkshire completely misunderstood his description of the city and its geography. To quote: "Edmonton is located on the Western Canadian prairies, close to the foothills of the Rocky Mountains."

Any English schoolboy glued to one of those new, twelve-inch black and white television screens of the mid-fifties knew all about the North American West! We'd all seen Gene Autry, Roy Rogers, the Lone Ranger, and a good half-dozen other cowboy heroes roaming those same western prairies! We knew exactly what was there: desert, miles and miles of it, full of towering cacti, mesas and ravines and endless craggy hills, and of course coyotes and longhorn cattle wandering free under an endless sun, probably alongside the deer and the antelope. In the distance would be the tall, Alp-like peaks of the Rockies, which were probably still topped with snow even in June. And finally, we all knew about North American cities full of enormous skyscrapers and twisting turnpikes.

Ah, yes ... Edmonton. This rapidly growing city sat amid thousands of acres of flat green farmland and endless poplar bush, everything connected by a web of gravel roads and the city itself dominated by a single six-storey "skyscraper". Edmonton was a huge disappointment, but other events, with a single exception, quickly made up for any real regret.

Summer wore on, hot and dry, and like any young lad on school holidays, I spent July and August searching for things to do. The home my parents had rented was the main floor of an up-and-down duplex in an area of Edmonton called Allendale. It was full of people with foreign-sounding names, and everyone seemed to get along just fine. Certainly the kids did. Curiously enough, my future wife—whom I would eventually meet in another part of the city—was eleven years old at the time, and lived only five blocks away.

A German family rented the upper floor of our newly built two-storey duplex. The man of the house had been a junior NCO serving in the Wehrmacht. My father was an ex-staff sergeant in the British army. They compared stories, and all animosity was clearly a thing of the past—except, perhaps, for the war between the alien, pungent smell of sauerkraut that regularly permeated the entire building, and that of our traditional roast lamb and Yorkshire pudding smothered in dark gravy and mint sauce.

Our area of town was a microcosm of Canada's early multicultural societies. My new friends had names such as Gruber and Hoffman; Elzheimer and Poppick; Secora and Markowski. These names mingled with the more familiar McCreavey, Brown, Smith, and Murray, plus a Higgitt from Wigan who arrived a year later and became my best friend. The amusing aspect of this mixture was that most of them had been in Edmonton for quite some time, and I was the only kid with an accent, a distinctly Yorkshire one. At first this did cause a paradoxical difficulty. Though freshly arrived from the land where the English language evolved, I was the only one whose speech everyone had trouble understanding.

Everything was so new and exciting, which was a great help in my adjustment after what was a major destabilization of a youngster's life. The summer of 1956 was full of seemingly endless sunshine that fell upon wooden sidewalks, gravel roads, new construction sites, the Edmonton Exhibition, trips to the lake, and at least a dozen new-found friends with whom I roamed the neighbourhood at will. The entertainment was familiar and fun: homemade pull-carts, marbles, hide and seek, playing at war, and the inevitable cowboys and Indians. Weather permitting, we were out all day—which meant nearly every day.

The Canadian kids seemed to have a lot more freedom, and certainly didn't lack creativity, such as manufacturing their makeshift "guns" using the scraps gleaned from the new construction sites that abounded just to the south of us. A couple feet of discarded one-inch tongue and groove plank could be carved into the rough shape of a rifle, the thin groove on top serving as a convenient channel for the "barrel." The "bullet" was a narrow strip of wooden shingle six to eight inches long, the width cut down to half an inch at the thick end of the shingle (the front of the "bullet") and an inch and a half at the thin end. The latter acted like a feather at the rear of an arrow. The resulting missile slid neatly into the groove on top of our "gun," and was propelled by an inch-wide circle of rubber cut from a car's inner tube. This was nailed to the end of the "barrel," where it was left to dangle when not in use.

To arm the weapon, we stretched the circle of rubber back along the groove and caught it in the jaws of a clothespin, nailed there to serve as the trigger. The narrow, carved shingle was then placed immediately in front of the now taut rubber band. Our makeshift weapon was then aimed at the friend or enemy of choice before pressing our thumbs down on the back of the clothespin to fire. Should the missile strike its target, the next step was to run.

The construction and use of those arrow guns was never questioned by our parents—until one of us inevitably struck someone else on a body part considered dangerous. This was nearly always the face. The resulting stream of blood brought a hysterical mother onto the street, yelling her head off. A forced, unilateral disarmament followed. By the next school break, however, all the hysterics were long forgotten by everyone in the neighbourhood including the kids, and the cycle would be repeated.

Ah, what the children of today miss while they're stuck in front of their computers!

The summer of 1956 was a tremendous experience for a newly arrived immigrant, but there were one or two hurdles that tarnished the glitter of my new country. As the proverb might well read, every silver lining has its cloud. My first problem was shared by almost anyone torn from their home environment: homesickness! By the end of August, when I was preparing to register for school, it had well and truly set in. Homesickness is a condition not to be underestimated, especially if another hurdle is dragging hard on a person's mind.

The heavy ache deep inside the gut and the chest is as physically real and solid as a sour-apple stomach ache. Mine would last until almost Christmas, compounded by the slow realization that friends "back home" were getting on with their lives without me. They did not, in fact, seem to know I existed anymore. The volume of much awaited letters "from home," written on the ten cent aero-grams available in those days, gradually slowed down as the months passed. Eventually they dried up. Or, to be blunt, *my* promptly written replies, one by one, gradually became unanswered. It was the only time in my life I regretted the move to Canada, and fortunately it was short-lived. A few months of self-inflicted misery was a small price to pay.

That "second hurdle", when put together with the homesickness, perhaps made that brief period of misery that much more acute—although a person can never be sure. One never knows the answers to any speculative "what if" question about the past, because it's impossible to do things over again and discover what might have been. Besides, it's pointless. As my grandmother would have said, a person should not dwell on what might have been; they should instead learn from what was. That's great advice, and maybe one day I'll find the self-discipline to take it.

The other hurdle that summer was my father. Toward the end of July, or at the latest the beginning of August, he completely rewrote the rules of parenting.

Chapter Two

My father is no longer who he seems to be …

As far back as I can remember, my father worked as an auto body repairman, though in England those so qualified went by the quaint name of panel beaters. His trade was originally that of blacksmith, which usually conjures an image of an enormous, burly male with muscular arms and barrel chest. My father certainly was not. Like me, he was of average height and build, and while fit enough, he probably never had to put iron shoes on a ton and a half of nervous horseflesh. When he qualified as a blacksmith, which would have been in the mid-1930s, forging iron rods into horseshoes on a red-hot forge was by then on its way out.

Born in 1917, Father would have been eligible for the draft when it was introduced in May of 1939, less than four months before war was declared. He likely volunteered because he joined up when the war was in its early stages, and his home was on Fulford Road, just down from the city's army barracks. (Of the 4,600,000 British military personnel who enrolled throughout the war, 1,400,000 were volunteers.) Father's trade qualification got him posted to the Royal Army Service Corps (RASC), Motor

Transport, and his war service was in North Africa, Sicily and Italy. Who knows, his trade and subsequent assignment to the RASC may have saved his life, in that he wasn't drafted into the PBI—the poor bloody infantry. If so, then I guess it probably saved mine too, simply by getting to be born.

Nearly seven years of RASC service would certainly have prepared him for the auto repair business by the end of the war, for as far as I know he took up "panel beating" when he was demobilized in 1946 as a staff sergeant. Using the words "as far as I know" makes me realize that there are a thousand questions that I should have asked when young, not only of parents, but of grandparents and even great-grandparents, for I can recall four of the latter. But alas, it's all too late, and the tradition continues. Our own children don't seem particularly interested in the past, at least not at this point in their lives, and by the time they are ... well, history will just repeat itself.

Father's choice of panel beating would have been a blessing to most young males, and it certainly was for me. As a kid I hung around the body shop in England, and later as a Canadian teenager anticipating an early driver's licence, such an environment was only a few steps short of paradise. There is an atmosphere in a garage that fascinates many young males, and I was no exception. The experience is probably akin to working inside a livery barn in the nineteenth century. Horses, cars—they surely hold a similar masculine appeal: a sleek, spirited horse and a fast, well-tuned car; the time spent training such an animal and the endless tinkering on that car; and there was doubtless a similar youthful strutting that came with the pride of ownership, regardless of the age and condition of either "beast." Beauty, after all, lies just as much in the eye of an owner as that of a beholder.

A similar comparison might also be drawn between these two distinctive businesses, a comparison that goes far beyond the basic function of keeping transport on the road. As with a horse barn, a garage has its own sharp, distinctive odour, though to youths who revel in such delights it is better called a delicious scent. The stale grease, the exotic smell of paint, the clinging fog of exhaust fumes, and the tantalizing pong of paint thinner—these smells surely hold the same allure as was once captured by the sweet scent of newly cut hay, the pungent aroma of fresh horse manure, and the unique, heady smell of horseflesh, best enjoyed when the nose is pressed hard against the soft hair of the animal's neck.

In short, I spent a lot of time in the auto body shops where my father worked and it was all voluntary—or at least it had been in England. In Canada I was also allowed to visit The Bump Shop, even though the business was not my father's own. It employed only a few men for it wasn't a large shop, but there were a lot of things a boy could find to keep himself busy. At first it was fun. Working around cars was never a chore, much like the old adage once offered by one of our local farmers where I now live: anyone who truly loves his job never has to work a lick in his life. It was far more enjoyable than remaining at home and working alongside Mother. While watching her peel potatoes a few years before, which looked like a really neat thing to do, I naively asked her if I could try. Big mistake! A couple tons of spuds later ...

The work schedule at the shop was forty-four hours a week, with the last four scheduled on a Saturday morning. Not everyone worked that day, and this was perhaps a way that my father could put in the extra four hours without the owner paying him time and a half. Whatever the reason, the Saturday visits, so briefly enjoyed that first July, soon became an event to dread.

Just the two of us were in the shop that Saturday, and I would guess it was not long past noon and time to go home. That meant the usual ritual of washing hands, forearms, and faces in preparation to leave.

The grime in the shop was mostly a fine paint dust that clung to the skin like a thin, multi-hued coating of flour. Our clothing attracted the more icky stuff such as a thick rainbow of paint stains, invisible needles of steel filings, clay-like streaks of body filler, and tiny holes from the red-hot sparks of the acetylene welders. The work was so hard on the clothes that the auto industry found it necessary to supply its employees with dungarees that were a sort of uniform. These came from Canadian Linen Supply, a company that delivered a combination of shirts and pants made from a faded green, twill-like material. This clothing was returned to Canadian Linen on a rotating, weekly basis for laundering. The garments were sent back clean, though still dotted with a myriad of ingrained paint stains and webs of zigzag stitching that closed the numerous rips and the larger charred holes.

The washroom at the back of the shop where we cleaned up is imprinted on my mind like a photograph. A chipped, chrome-rimmed mirror greeted all who walked in, fixed to the wall above a paint-splotched, wall-mounted porcelain sink that would never sparkle again no matter how well it was scrubbed. Beside it sat a similarly splotched porcelain toilet with a permanent stain at the water level. Alongside was a limp, rotating cloth towel that hung in a grey loop from a holder that was screwed to plasterboard walls yellowing with age. The walls were painted only by an artist's palette of colourful paint streaks, left there by dozens of sticky, hastily wiped hands. Almost forgot: the toilet paper sat on top of the toilet tank, usually a couple of rolls at a time, and often crinkled from the water that splashed from the nearby sink.

There was no need to close the door when I went in that day, for I was simply washing my hands. There was nothing odd about my father wandering in either, because he needed to wash his hands too. However, on this particular Saturday, instead of joining me at the sink, he did something that he had never done before. He casually unbuttoned his fly and began to urinate.

Now, this was taking place maybe a foot off to my right, and it was most unusual. In fact, he had never done such a thing in my life. Unless in the company of your younger peers, taking a pee was a private event, and even then it was usually behind a bush or you at least turned your back. In the presence of an adult, however, the privacy was almost a ritual. Such an event nearly always took place in a men's public toilet, all of which seemed to operate under an unwritten law of nature. Each male would assiduously study whatever faceless wall stood a foot in front of his nose, pretending he was the only one in the room. Yet now, here was my father brazenly standing beside me with his willie hanging out!

My eyes remained glued to the grubby mirror above the sink.

"Have you done anything with it yet?"

Silence. *Concentrate on the mirror.*

Nothing more was said as I finished washing. We used a commercial soap to get rid of the grimed-in dirt, a grease-like, orange-brown substance that looked and felt like finely gritted furniture polish. I quickly rinsed off whatever remained of the sparse lathery goo, eager to get away. The towel rack was on the wall on the far side of my father, though, and for a moment I stood there dripping water, my eyes still on the sink.

The splash of urine finally ended and the small room fell eerily silent. A shadow of movement came from somewhere off to my right, and I'm sure Father was casually flicking the darned thing up and down. Then, "You know what I mean—have you started playing with it?"

***

In fact, no, I didn't know what he meant. The closest I'd ever been to "playing with it" was in primary school, maybe third grade, when some of us chose the long, open-trough urinal in the boys' toilet to measure how far we could "shoot." The reason I remember that event—and can't resist recounting it—is because this soon led to seeing who could run under the arching spouts of urine. The game ended when I ran dry and laid a stripe across another boy's shoulders. The lad, whose name is long forgotten, promptly ran off and told the nearest teacher that Graham had peed on his back.

The summons didn't take long. Report to one of the school's six classrooms, where half a dozen teachers were still enjoying their tea break. I can still remember Mrs. Santon, standing tall beside the window with a teacup in one hand and a cigarette in the other as the facts were laid at her feet. I was terrified.

Thinking back with an adult's perspective, it was amazing how they all managed to keep straight faces. *A stripe of urine across another kid's back? Just when we thought we'd heard everything! How on earth ... ?*

I told all, and there was no punishment. But then, why would there have been? The event was probably the teachers' best chuckle of the week.

But as to my father's question, what he meant by "playing with it" was truly a mystery. Incredible as it may sound today, even at the age of thirteen, I had no idea what he was talking about, and I don't believe that was unusual. A lot of kids of my acquaintance in the fifties, either still twelve or just breaking into their teens, were babes in the woods compared to the youngsters of today. At the time, what little sex education I *had* received consisted of a vague lecture, and not long after, a little understood "dirty" joke. Both were puzzling because each lacked the essential details, such as related body parts, how to use them, and why you'd bother to do so in the first place. Like the faltering golden arch in the boys' toilet, just about everything had flown over my head.

The vague lecture, which turned out to be truly ironic, was my father's "birds and the bees" talk the previous summer in England. Allan, a friend of mine, had asked me if I would like to go camping with him and his parents. The impromptu lecture was somehow meant to tell me why I couldn't go. It was prolonged and rambling, finally homing in on thousands and thousands of tadpole-like creatures that swam vigorously up a mysterious stream that existed somewhere off in the ether. This frantic trek apparently took place in order to meet up with a tiny egg embedded in a sort of ethereal cloud at the stream's end. The egg waited there in solitary splendour, its sole purpose to glom onto one of the tadpoles and magically become a baby. And no, they were not like chicken eggs, they were just sort of very small eggs the size of a speck of grit ...

Yeah, right. But what about Allan and the camping trip?

Unfortunately, my father failed to describe the physiology as the tadpoles set out on their long, suicidal swim (all but one would die, I did get that part, but there was no mention of a penis, sperm, or coital sex). He also neglected to mention the route the tadpoles had to follow (the vagina). As a result, that part of the lecture remained a mystery and quite frankly, I wasn't interested enough to ask for more details. I wasn't particularly interested in how babies were made either, because all I wanted was to go camping with my friend, Allan. Even so, I suppose I'd gained some knowledge at that point: babies came from things that look like tadpoles, and thousands and thousands of them die while searching for an egg the size of a speck of grit.

Once the delicate part of the talk was over and done with, the truly ironic part followed. It was an equally vague talk about the evil things that can happen to little boys if they go away with someone else's father—again, with none of the finer details provided (what a bloody hypocrite). So I remained completely baffled on all counts, other than the bottom line. I couldn't go camping with my friend, Allan; tadpoles didn't always turn into frogs; and I'd missed out on a great holiday for no good reason at all.

The second lesson on sexual reproduction occurred at school, perhaps a few months following the strange lecture on tadpoles, and it contained far more grist. Bypassing all the useless details received so far, it homed in on the basics: how that baby got inside a woman's stomach in the first place. To be honest, this was a mystery that I'd simply never questioned, probably because it held no interest to me at the time. Even so, it was someone at school who saw fit to fill me in, albeit in a backhanded sort of way. A classmate called Irwin (that was his surname, we never used Christian names once we were through primary school) told a tired, juvenile joke:

"If your mum and dad had an argument, who would you stick up for?" he asked.

"I dunno."

"You'd stick up for your dad, silly, because he stuck up for you."

"Huh?"

"You know, because your dad *stuck up* for you!"

"Er ..." Embarrassed silence, then, "I don't get it."

Irwin patiently provided the basic, unbelievable details of sexual intercourse. Yet even he didn't (or perhaps couldn't) explain why a man might want to do such an odd thing with his willie in the first place. Just as important, he gave no reason why a woman would want to let him, though I took that answer for granted. She would have to let him do it if she wanted a baby, wouldn't she? That's Logic 101.

Irwin made no mention of sperm, either, and certainly nothing about pleasure, and I've since wondered if his mind also became bogged down in mystery at that point. There was no mention of tadpoles, of course, so that part of it never came up. I was curious enough to ask around and confirm Irwin's explanation, mainly by repeating the joke in a knowing manner. But once it was verified, I simply stashed away the facts as one more useless tidbit of information on the mysterious world of adults.

And further to my father's prying question that Saturday at The Bump Shop, none of the boys I knew until then had ever said a word about playing with himself. Nor had anyone even hinted at what that involved, or why a lad would do so in the first place. Not that we boys were totally innocent. I think we'd all had our go at playing doctor, though that was at a younger age, when the girls were just as curious, definitely more obliging, and equally naive. And by the time we turned thirteen, we had definitely started to notice those same girls, especially the budding bits. But as far as I and my two closest friends were concerned, similar naifs called Lewis and Greenwood, that was as far as it went. Of course, at thirteen we probably would have given our right arm to play doctor again, if we ever got the chance—even if we still didn't know *why* we wanted to play doctor. All we knew was that it would be exciting as hell to have another sly peek.

***

"Here," my father said in the body shop washroom. A hand fell on my wrist, pulling it sideways. "Just hold it firm, like that." The same hand shifted to cover my hand, and both started moving together.

This is all wrong. Even though I knew nothing about what was happening here, there was an instinctive sense of *wrong*.

"Good, that's good—now—just keep moving your hand back and forth, like this ..."

My mind went sort of numb, a sullen mood darkened my brain, a brain that had become strangely detached—or maybe semi-detached, because it was impossible to detach it completely.

"Yes, that's it, let me help—there—that's better—"

My eyes watched but my mind remained numb, wondering, *What is the point of this? What is happening? How long does this have to go on? It just isn't right...*

My father's whole body stiffened. His hand tightened over mine as he suddenly gasped, and an odd, blank expression appeared on his face. Something strange was happening, and I quickly pulled my hand free of his. He murmured something I can't remember, if I even heard it to begin with, and suddenly there were spurts of white fluid dripping into the grimy toilet bowl.

Confused, totally confused as to what had just happened, I stood there, as did my father, his trousers now slumped about his ankles. I didn't remember seeing them get there.

Then he turned on the tap, waited for the water to warm, and picked up an old bar of soap that was so dry it had dark cracks along its length. He rubbed it between his palms under the water, and eventually it began to lather. Neither of us said a word.

More rubbing of soap, more lather, then he turned to face me, his palms full of soapsuds. Shaking his left hand free of the suds, he reached out to tug at my belt. It took but a second for the buckle to come free, even as I stood there wondering what was happening.

And I didn't do anything. Nothing! This was my father. I'd spent the last thirteen years doing exactly what he told me to do. So I did nothing but stand there as he did what he was doing.

Even if I wanted to describe what happened next, it would be impossible. I simply don't remember the precise details, other than the strange, oddly pleasant sensation that surged through my entire body just before everything was over and done. That sudden sensation was a complete shock that I promptly shunted to the back of my mind to deal with later. I simply stood there in silence, my trousers now in the same position as those of my father—who suddenly turned all bright and breezy.

"Come on, we'd better be going home. Mum will be wondering where we are."

What just happened? What was it all about?

And what, exactly, was that weird sensation?

I numbly reached down, pulled up my trousers and organized myself, stealing a sidelong glance at my father, who was tucking in his shirt. Though he was just of average height I had to look up, for I was probably only about five foot two or three at the time. Even when I hit sixteen, my first driver's licence described me as five foot six and 140 pounds, which meant I had a bit more than three inches to grow. I was always a late developer—in more ways than one, I suppose.

A thousand thoughts were bouncing through my mind, and contained inside one of them was a question that just might provide a sane answer to this dreadful feeling of wrongness. In fact, there was only one, single answer that could make this entire episode right with my world.

"Do all fathers do this with their sons, Dad?"

I clearly remember asking the question, just as surely as I remember the answer. Certain events stick like glue.

My father smiled, a *humph* sort of smile that came from one side of his mouth. "No, I don't think so." He paused, plainly amused. "I suppose you could say I'm sort of special."

This answer seemed to prompt a further comment, probably the classic one-liner of the pedophile. "You shouldn't tell anyone about this, though. They might not understand."

I already knew that, without being told. Hell, I wasn't going to tell a soul!

I would also guess that's the classic one-line reaction of the pedophile's victim. It's what child abusers rely on.

CHAPTER THREE

My father: who he was, and who he could have been ...

C hristened Grenville Rex, my father always went by his middle name, which also happens to be my middle name, though I have never used it. (Had I been christened Grenville, though, I might well have). Father was an intelligent man, a gift that extended primarily to the practical things in life. He never received further education beyond his trade, and while he did read, he was far from being a bookworm. He was adept in many areas besides the trade that gave him his living, however, and he could be quite creative. In other words, he would make a decent job of whatever he chose to do, often starting from scratch.

There was a piece that was frequently missing, however—the one that is best called common sense. This is not unusual in people possessed of above average smarts. There is a book titled *Why Smart People Do Dumb Things*, by Mortimer Feinberg, PhD, that could have readily devoted a full chapter to my father's foibles, and this is without even mentioning the pedophilia. His "everyday" personality flaws may have been fuelled from many sources: ego, misplaced confidence (or lack of confidence), plain selfishness (surely, by definition, pedophilia is at the top of the "selfish" list), and who knows what else, including how he was raised by his parents before him. Psychologists can better tell us why we do dumb things, though not always how to stop doing them. With Father, the bottom line was a compulsive need for others to think well of him—which in fairness is a trait common to most of us, though fortunately to a far lesser degree. To resort to the vernacular, Dad had a deep-seated need to "play the man."

Having spent a lifetime dealing with many successful (and unsuccessful) people, a few observations have been made along the way. One is that there are many positive characteristics that we strive for, and not always with success. Some of the most desirable, though unfortunately not always the most sought-after qualities, are wisdom, common sense, compassion, intelligence, and above all, plain human decency. Of these basic traits, only intelligence appears to be an inherent absolute. In other words, you either have it or you don't. The other desirable characteristics, which are far more crucial to a satisfying life, must be achieved. And the point as it relates to Father? Intelligence often seems to act as a stumbling block in gaining these more beneficial traits.

Father's need to be well thought of by others caused the most strife between my parents, beginning very early in their marriage. Picking up the tab, being ostentatious, and keeping up appearances was a role that cost money, and money was always short. As the marriage wore on, his attention grew less focused on the hard details of running the business, on his family, and on Mother herself—which we constantly heard about from a very early age. Mother always told all. Father's particular stumbling block in Canada was not learning lessons from the past, primarily the causes of his prior failures.

To be specific, in coming to Canada, Father had found a decent job. It offered a regular paycheque, the bills were (initially) paid on time, and for awhile things at home seemed to be settled, at least at the financial level. The family enjoyed summer holidays camping at Pigeon Lake, money was available for minor treats such as movies and the odd day out, and there would soon be a house. However, Father was an employee, and an employee is not the man in charge!

Oddly enough, my profession has helped me to understand at least a part of this. There is a certain kind of independence in being self-employed, and a pride in this sort of self-sufficiency. Sometimes an inflated self-image also comes with being in charge as it truly did with Father, but that attitude is far from universal. I've also noticed over the years that a high percentage of my self-employed clients were raised by at least one self-employed parent. Heck, I was self-employed too, just like my father. Maybe it is something that's simply passed on.

My father worked at The Bump Shop for more than a year and a half, and I assume he left because he wanted to. As an aside, in writing about these events, I find myself wondering if there were other reasons for him leaving there, too, just as I have come to wonder about his reasons for leaving England. If so, they were never discussed. And if not, maybe it's just latent paranoia finally rising to the surface. Regardless of the reasons, Father set up a shop of his own in 1958, and called it Crown Auto Body.

The operation was nearly always busy enough to keep two auto body men as well as my father in work, yet the profits never seemed to stick. Ever the terrible businessman, he never kept track of the paperwork, often underbid to get a job (understandable, but fatal—an object lesson learned later in life when observing my less fortunate accounting clients), and when he had cash in hand he seemed to fritter it away. These poor business practices helped speed the onset of yet another financial crisis, one that, with straight thinking, Father could have avoided. He kept things going for three or four years, then again went bankrupt in late 1961 or early 1962. As it turned out, in the long run and strictly from a financial point of view, this was probably the best thing that could have happened for everyone concerned... at the time.

More than a lack of business acumen caused the failure, however. On the personal side, he frequented a bathhouse located in downtown Edmonton for a period during this time, as did one of his employees. This establishment had the typical seedy reputation also attributed to the bathhouses in New York and San Francisco (if you've got time on your hands, read *And The Band Played On*, Randy Shilts, St. Martin's Press; part of the book deals with the role these bathhouses played in the initial rapid spread of Aids and some of the statistics are startling, to say the least). No doubt some of the cash, perhaps a lot of it, went that way too—along with time spent that might have been given to his family. Not that the latter lack was all bad—as far as I was concerned, the less time he spent with me during that period, the better.

Father was in his mid-forties when Crown Auto Body went under, and a brief description of his appearance and interests might help to show more of his character, and the first impression he might instill. Rex Clews was a striking man. Attractive, even as a child, he aged well, holding his looks (relatively) until well into his eighties. Though he stood just five foot eight, he was well-proportioned and never overweight. His fair hair was wavy, his eyes were blue, his otherwise straight nose bore a small bump from an early break, and he had a firm, cleft chin. When I was about sixteen, a girl I was dating made an unusual comment for a teenager, considering Father was then a middle-aged man: "Wow, is your dad ever good-looking."

Whereas women found him quite attractive, hindsight reminds me that he showed no particular interest. Not that he didn't welcome the attention, but he seemed to find it more amusing than anything else. Mother certainly never complained when it happened, nor did she appear to be worried that he might stray. Just the opposite, actually, because she often complained about Father's lack of marital interest, along with the flip comment that if someone else could get him interested, they were more than welcome. It was sarcasm, of course, but that was Mother. Even so, did she instinctively know that his interests lay, to say the least, elsewhere? Sure, he caught a woman's attention, but that was almost laughable, considering he was an active pedophile. And, what with visiting the down town baths with his employee, he was no doubt a practicing homosexual, at least in those earlier years.

But all of that was a part of Father's darker side. Nearly all humans have a darker side, it's just a matter of how dark it becomes. With Father, parts of it got pretty damned black. But nearly everyone also has their upside, and my father had his fair share of positive points, too. Just like the rest of us, he tried to keep the positive side on display, and most of the faults out of sight. Yet there is an irony in this. It seems that minor character flaws within a person are almost impossible to hide, while major flaws can be very well concealed, especially those that occur behind closed doors, such as pedophilia. This was something Father managed to do for a phenomenally long period of time. As mentioned before, did he do this in England, as well?

Because he ran a business in York, a city that in the fifties had a population of around a hundred thousand, Father was more than likely reasonably well-known. This recognition was no doubt enhanced by his voice, a resonant tenor that promised more to come. Before leaving England he was a member of the York Male Voice Choir, performing at least two solos at every concert. He even sang at my wedding. He cut a single record, a seventy-eight, which has unfortunately become lost to time.

Father did well in the various singing competitions he entered, usually giving voice to the more well-known Italian arias. He would often take Mother and me along, and it was exciting to go and listen. My mind still drifts back in time when hearing such pieces as *La donna e mobile* and *Your tiny hand is frozen*, two of his favourites—and mine. The judges always remarked on the quality of his voice, even if he just placed rather than won. The comments were kind and always included the suggestion that he would go far if he took lessons and had his career properly promoted. That, however, required discipline and money and support at home, all of which were lacking.

On the other hand, thank whatever gods that be for things turning out that way—and I don't mean only for the family, but for Father himself. It's a nightmare to think of what would have happened—one way or another—if he had ever made it big! I mean, just think of one of the famous tenors turning out to be a pedo ...

No, let's not go there.

My real purpose in describing Father is this: he was not an unfortunate Quasimoto with a chip on one shoulder and an axe to grind. He had the looks, the brains, and the voice—and he had all the opportunity of a promising career in many fields. Unfortunately, of the five desirable character traits listed earlier, he only had one in abundance—innate intelligence—which proved to be never enough to latch onto any of the other, more desirable qualities. As with many people of such ilk, I don't think he even tried. Maybe such goals should be taught in school, and placed well ahead of simply being smart. Heck, the Greeks attempted as much a few thousand years ago, and yet we like to think we're progressive.

What Father was capable of, yet did not achieve ... well, who knows—but what a waste!

CHAPTER FOUR

The first year in Canada, one of much learning …

The first home we rented in Edmonton had three bedrooms and covered the entire main floor of the up-and-down duplex. The building still stands, with little exterior change. The upstairs suite where the German family lived was self-enclosed, only accessible through the rear door of the building. Just inside this doorway the stairway led directly upward from a small hallway that also served as a landing for another set of stairs that went down to the undeveloped basement. This layout left one of our three bedrooms isolated beyond the back door of our family suite. This became my bedroom, while my two younger sisters and our now ten-month-old brother Steve all shared a second bedroom next to that of my parents. This was the most sensible arrangement, considering the relative ages of the kids. I soon began to hate it.

As those balmy days of summer crept by I naively hoped that the incident at The Bump Shop was a one-time learning experience—perhaps a weird, real-life extension of the tadpole lecture I received in England. It was a forlorn hope, admittedly, but not an unreasonable one at the time for an optimistic thirteen-year-old mind. It seems that so many things in life are "not that unreasonable at the time."

On the positive side, finding myself suddenly alone in that isolated rear bedroom did give me the opportunity to enjoy the single benefit of that first, shameful episode with my father. That strange, shuddering feeling at the end of the encounter was like nothing I'd ever experienced, and it was time to find out if the sensation was permanent. I did this in great secrecy, of course, and with the uneasy feeling that in some manner this sort of thing was also shamefully wrong—but not nearly wrong enough to stop doing it! The experience, along with the results, also provided the final piece of an old jigsaw puzzle, missing since Irwin told his feeble joke. It slowly dawned on me where those damned tadpoles hung out—plus it clearly explained the mystery of why a boy was willing to do such an odd thing to a girl with his 'willie'. (It would still take a while longer to figure out why that same girl might actually be willing to let him).

Fortunately, young boys do talk to each other, and on that particular topic, talk we did. Over the following six months or so it came as quite a surprise to learn that all my newfound buddies were also "doing it," which certainly lowered the inherent guilt. It's funny that when the question did crop up in our small group—and it was certainly a popular issue at the time—there was no hesitation in 'fessing up, though we were universally shy on the ethics of what we were doing. Bear in mind we were only twelve or thirteen, and all of us to some degree were haunted by an uneasy feeling that we might well be wallowing in sin. A few were even a bit worried that there were only so many "shots" in it, or it might wear out early with too much use, though I don't think any of us thought we were in danger of going blind. And despite all these hotly debated concerns, none of us were bothered enough to lose sleep over it—not once we got to sleep, anyway.

Along with this newfound "coming of age" rite (no pun intended, but it's there anyway) came a standard challenge from the other boys: "Are you producing yet?" This manly passage led to a rather amusing incident at my friend Tom's house. Eddie, the youngest of our not-so-innocent-now group, was challenged on exactly this issue, along with a few jeers and hoots of disbelief when his reply was a defensive, "Yeah, I am." Not to be outdone by his older peers who plainly didn't believe him, he went behind the door in Tom's bedroom and came out two minutes later with a rather meagre-looking palm full of proof.

Why the rather graphic anecdote? Despite suddenly becoming a victim of sexual abuse, to all outward appearances, my life continued as normal—whatever normal was for a bunch of thirteen-year-old boys in those days. And such "off the wall" chat *was* considered normal for boys of that age, for we were kids who were disarmingly open with each other in a society that was staid and closeted by today's standards. As to what we were all doing in the privacy of our spare time, well, that was normal too. There was a saying we all used at one time or another back then, perhaps as justification for our self-inflicted guilt: hey, nine out of ten boys whack off anyway, and the tenth is a liar.

Having said that, every last one of us would have been utterly shocked to have discovered that the objects of our fantasies were also "doing it." I believe the now ancient Kinsey Report put the level at around two-thirds of the female population—though how many of the other unsullied third were also liars is open to guess. Nonetheless, this may have been the sole area of statistical endeavour that we boys were truly ahead of the girls.

***

Unfortunately, it wasn't long before the other, inadmissible side of life resumed its sullen new pattern. Any hope of The Bump Shop incident being a one-time lesson on the facts of life quickly disappeared. Less than a week after the incident, shortly after falling asleep, I was awakened by a knocking on my bedroom door. The irony that anyone had to knock on my bedroom door at all was because my father, with the bedroom being outside the apartment proper, had replaced the old door knob with one that had a lock on it in order to "keep me safe."

The knocking came from Father, of course. He quickly came inside, urging me to be quiet in a hushed voice, even as he locked the door and dropped his pyjama bottoms. I presumed Mother was asleep, though as time passed that notion proved to be questionable. Just how many times can a man leave his bed in the middle of the night without being noticed? And when noticed, wouldn't his wife ask where on earth he was going, and why? Might she not even follow and at least listen, if for no other reasons than curiosity and concern? Yet those nocturnal visits to the isolated bedroom continued regularly over the following year, and Mother never mentioned them at all.

Father didn't waste any time, that first night. What followed was little different from what had happened at The Bump Shop. I remained silent and surly throughout all the back and forth fumbling, an attitude that I recall distinctly. This sullen demeanour instantly became the norm, even as I did as instructed. And why wouldn't I? There should never be a need for an abused child to make excuses, yet even now I find myself again pointing out that for thirteen years I had been firmly taught to do as I was told.

The only option available then seemed to be passive resistance, or perhaps a more modern term, deliberate noncompliance. Call it the Gandhi option. I resolved from the outset not to respond to anything my father did to me, a stance that in some ways was not truly a conscious decision, but automatic. A dark gloom would instantly block my mind, starting with the first knock on that damned door.

(Again, where was mother while this was going on?)

As time passed, this base sullenness became normal. I would pout and clam up and will my mind to be elsewhere, but this never seemed to bother my father. Who knows, maybe it encouraged him. At first I laboured under the belief that a grim, surly attitude might eventually make him quit. It never occurred to me that he might find it a turn-on, yet as I write this down, I wonder if perhaps it was.

As to the other side in these humiliating encounters, namely me, it was hopeless to try to prevent a final climax despite what anyone might claim to the contrary. A sullen, uncooperative mind might well try to command the body, but the body will go ahead and do whatever it damn-well pleases. Some people may not believe that, but it's true.

I remember reading, maybe thirty years ago, about a rape that had taken place in England. A woman had broken up with her boyfriend and found a new love. For whatever unimaginable reason, the girl and her new boyfriend decided it would be a good lark to kidnap the old beau, take him to a cottage and tie him to a bed, where she agreed to rape him. There was little in the article about her first boyfriend, but he certainly wasn't keen on the idea. He may have been a bit of a prude, or perhaps his only sin was possession of a good, upright set of moral standards. I don't know what the legal outcome was, but as a rape victim he laid charges.

Oh boy! Like it or not, there is a double standard in the public's view of an adult sexual assault. (How many women initially found the Linda Bobbit case to be a bit of a giggle?) When this same English rape case came to the attention of a friend of mine, a professional woman, she and several other women made it the subject of a casual lunchtime discussion. Several thought the episode was actually hilarious. Nearly all of them claimed it was physically impossible for a woman to rape a man. A couple did suggest there was an outside chance it could be done, though the reason offered was the old dig about a man's brain and his penis not being connected. Bear in mind that all these ladies were independent women who would have voiced the opinion that a male rapist should, at the very least, have his sexual appendage removed with a blunt knife, with a slow death following soon after—probably by fire.

Notwithstanding their opinion, let me unequivocally discount their conclusion—the first part, about the physical impossibility of raping a man, not the penile connection to the brain. No matter how determined, no matter how focused, no matter where a male's mind is or how sullen and black his mood, that relatively small part of his body *will* respond to skillful manipulation, and eventually reach orgasm. Sexual response, let me assure you, can be purely physical, with no willing participation by the mind. And while even I must confess to some amusement on first hearing of the above incident, I can also assure you that if the background story was indeed true, that male in the news article was actually raped.

On the other hand—and I'll state it now, having been subject to a somewhat similar process over a period of two to three years—there is a balance. As the sexual abuse is occurring, you can divorce your mind from what is happening. In fact, I suspect that's more common than not with abused children, be the abuse sexual, physical or mental. And later, on a day to day basis when away from the abuse, it is possible for the flip side of this to kick in. A person, a kid, is also able to completely divorce the sexual abuse that has been inflicted, even the night before, from that other, everyday part of life that we like to call "normal."

A child's life must go on, after all, and indeed it usually does, because I think children are more resilient than most adults believe. Kids, for the most part, absorb what is going on, and they do their damnedest to adjust. That doesn't mean there isn't any psychological damage taking place, but most manage to adjust in some manner in order to keep going. It's called survival. Even to this day, none of my friends in junior or senior high school (and we still get together) had a hint of what was happening, nor did anyone else seem to have any idea, except Father—and in all probability, Mother. And indeed, why should they know about what was happening at home? Everything else was going fine. My hormones were kicking in big-time as my fourteenth birthday came and went, assisted by the fact that there were girls everywhere. I adjusted.

And did I adjust! I recall in particular the junior high graduation dance, held during our last week at school before hitting the big time: senior high school. The lights in the gym were low and the dances were slow and some of the boys started kissing the girls, or was it vice versa? Who cared? The teachers, surprisingly, didn't seem to mind, maybe because in a few more days we were no longer their problem anyway. In short order we were all necking on the dance floor, clinging to each other as the music oozed on. Oh yes, everything was going fine, thank you. Father's behaviour became a totally separate part of my life I found best to ignore, except on those days when I could not.

Sexual abuse is handled by victims each in their own way, dealing with it as they are able. My response was to try to ignore it. However, no matter how successful I believed I was with that, it was not the right thing to do. It is, in fact, a dreadfully wrong thing to do. In the long run it does nothing more than allow the pedophile to continue along his predatory path, while the victim muddles on with his or her emotional problems bottled up inside.

The long-term effects will surely differ greatly among children who are sexually abused, these effects being further divided between the two genders. Obviously, on a first-hand basis, I can only speak for myself and merely speculate on how it affects other boys. As to the girls, I suspect—no, I firmly believe, based on similar, albeit limited first-hand knowledge—that for them the long-term effects are far more damaging overall. Even so, with both genders, a surprising number of children do manage to soldier on even while the abuse is taking place, keeping this very private aspect of their life tucked away in a cubbyhole where no one but they and their abusers ever venture. And the net result, again, becomes the surpreme irony: these kids will keep their silence, thus ensuring continuing abuse!

Pedophiles rely on this. Surprisingly, they often do so without offering any overt or drastic threat. Threats do happen, but why should the abuser threaten, other than to caution his victim? To begin with, the child is usually burdened with undeserved shame, and almost certainly possessed by self inflicted guilt. And, as if that's not enough, the child also fears a whole series of events, most imaginary, that must surely ensue if the sexual abuse is revealed. Never mind the fear of publicity and shame, which is a terrible image in itself. The confused, abused child is also afraid that, by speaking out, he or she will predicate the destruction of their entire way of life. With the father in jail, the family structure will be blown apart, financial stability will be gone, friends will be lost and social life destroyed. And in the victim's mind there will erroneously dwell this message: *All this would be my fault, because I am the one who told.*

In the meantime, the pedophile continues along his destructive path. God only knows what's going on in his mind, particularly about the chances of being caught, for a logical person would say that it is inevitable. Only it isn't, and nobody knows the true statistics as to how many simply get away with it. After all, how do you get an accurate count of the number of ghosts you cannot see? Yet even if being caught proves inevitable, it still may take years to happen. And while those years are passing, the predator moves on to the raw, tragic excitement of his next encounter. The very risk of living this way must surely be a turn-on in itself.

Not that the young victim cares. Victims are too busy worrying about otherwise responsible adults knocking on their door in the middle of the night, and about having to live in the lonely silence of what follows. This is what, in the long run, makes so many of them such tough little devils.

CHAPTER FIVE

Life continues, as does everything else ...

We are creatures of habit. The family's initial move to the south side of Edmonton was based on the fact that The Bump Shop was also there, but we remained in various south side locations as long as we lived in our rapidly expanding city. Even when I married another "south-sider" some years later, we remained on the same side of the river until eventually moving away from Edmonton. All of us tend to feel more comfortable with the familiar, even when the road of familiarity grows rockier than the path of the strange and unknown. It's a trait that probably dates back to the Stone Age. It's a trait that also contributes to maintaining a status quo that sometimes doesn't deserve to continue. In other words, if one can adjust to and tolerate a situation that's survivable, this can feel more secure than jumping into an unknown that might actually prove to be far better. Kids in particular feel that way, because they are kids.

In mid-1957 our family rented another, larger home about half a block east of the first duplex. The basement was rented out, as was a small suite on the top floor. I believe my parents leased the entire house and sublet these two smaller units. Perhaps the move was a way of making a few extra dollars. Maybe the rent on the old place was in arrears and we had to move. Maybe the tenant upstairs at the old place got fed up with the whispers and door-knocking after midnight. Or maybe I've just become so paranoid over the years that I'm imagining there was a snake hiding under every rock.

We remained in this second home for a year, during which time I went to another school and completed grade ten. Unlike my previous bedroom, the new one was not separate from the rest of the suite. This meant my door had no lock, raising the prospect that Father's visits would cease. It was not to be. The knocking came to a halt, yes, but it was replaced by a not-too-subtle shaking of my shoulder in the middle of the night, when everyone else was, presumably, asleep. Then the usual stuff happened, mutual masturbation with hardly a whispered word. I would stare into the darkness with sullen indifference as my mind wandered off to the refuge of whatever haven it could conjure. Father would quietly grunt his satisfaction with my vacuous help, then turn the tables and insist on doing the same to me. Sharing the guilt?

It was early in that second year, or perhaps the latter half of the previous—it's so hard to remember exactly when—that my lack of response clearly began to irritate Father, though I don't think my surly moods were the real cause. In fact, it's quite possible that this sullenness formed part of his gratification, for he never attempted to force a change, which in retrospect was odd. Had such an attitude been displayed anywhere else, such as in the everyday 'normal' part of our lives, it would have never been tolerated. No, I think his irritation was due more to impatience, for it took forever to get the manual stimulus to work—though eventually it always did.

Whether annoyed, or bored, or maybe both, he introduced a new slant—he began to use his mouth. This was no instant solution by any means. In fact, I'm sure it took no less time to complete the act than it did manually. Perhaps it simply gave him an extra sort of gratification, who knows? Regardless of reason, this soon became the normal practice, but for one, single exception.

Right after this new routine began, he tried to get me to do it to him. I was physically sick. I remember the awful gagging the moment things began, and whatever remains of dinner that still sat in my belly at one a.m. quickly wound up on the bed sheets. There really wasn't much left but a bunch of bits and bile, but it caused an instant flurry of soft curses, hasty cleanup of sour vomit, and firm instructions about what to say in the morning if Mother questioned the soiled linen—which she did. I said I'd been sick during the night from a bellyache, which she likely attributed to something I'd eaten. I suppose it damn-near was. On the other hand, though I wasn't aware of it at the time, I had begun to make excuses for my father's actions.

This episode did gave rise to two positive results, the first immediate, though short-lived. Father slunk back to join my mother and never did finish what he'd been there for, which was the first and only time that I recall that ever happening. And, more long-term, he never tried to do the same thing again. While that may sound strange, considering he'd wanted it done in the first place, he probably figured that it was beyond my tolerance level—which I suppose it was. At the time such a notion never struck me, though. All I felt was extreme relief.

Looking back, the fact that Father so readily abandoned an act he was clearly intent on doing should have made me realize that perhaps he could be resisted. If my balking at performing fellatio, even through the spontaneous act of being sick, would make him stop, then perhaps other means of resistance were possible. A more aggressive kid would probably have realized this. But then, a more aggressive kid might well have stopped the whole thing at the very beginning. (And again, where was Mother during all of this—she was not that sound a sleeper!)

A side story, this one about hypocrisy. Sometime during this period, a young newlywed couple took over the upstairs suite. The tiny apartment's bathroom held a toilet, a sink, and a very small shower, and my parents gave the couple permission to use our bathroom whenever they wanted a proper bath. One weekend afternoon they spent a half-hour or more in the tub—together. My parents were horrified—what a terrible example to set for the children! The couple was told never to do such an indecent thing again, or they would have to leave—by my angry father, no less! Again, there was that blatant hypocrisy.

Fortunately the bedroom visits in this second house soon came to an end, perhaps to some extent due to economics. My parents agreed to take in a young lodger at the request of one of their friends. Danny was a bachelor and I'd guess his age might have been around thirty—at fourteen it's hard to tell how old any adult is, because everyone over the age of eighteen is ancient and even sixteen is pushing the limit. The main floor of the house was not large and Danny moved into my room, after the addition of a second single bed. Rather than being resentful, which many kids my age might have been, I was greatly relieved. The nocturnal visits promptly ceased. The relief, however, was once again short-lived.

It was not long after Danny moved in that Father left The Bump Shop and began working at the new location that became known as Crown Auto Body. It was located in the Forest Heights district, several miles from where we lived. There was an interim takeover period of about six months, during which he worked as manager of the shop for a man called John Turgeon. I don't know what the arrangements were, but there was probably a profit incentive. Father had complete charge and he worked all hours, including weekends, when no other staff members were around. That was bad news for me, because it wasn't long before this body shop became a convenient new venue for the abuse.

There was one positive aspect to the move. Father decided that, as I was now moving toward fifteen, it was time to teach me a bit more about the auto body business. Under normal circumstances this would have been terrific. Right from day one, I was there on a regular basis—after school, on weekends, and during school holidays—this time doing real work. Over the next couple of years I began learning how to pound fenders, paint cars, and use an acetylene torch. Unfortunately, this also meant working alongside Father at the shop on weekends, as well as many evenings.

The summer of 1958 also saw my parents move their residence to Forest Heights, still on the south side of the river. The lot purchased for our home was hardly more than a block from Crown Auto Body, which was the reason for the move. The house was a small bungalow that was hauled onto the lot in a deal worked out with a distant relative. It turned out that my mother had a great-aunt living in the city, Auntie Madge, and her husband George Kilgour. They also resided on the south side on a corner lot situated on 99th Street, one of the main arteries leading to downtown Edmonton. (More than fifty years later, this street is still as congested as it was then.)

The mid-fifties were a very busy time out west, and a good deal of construction was taking place. The Kilgours' home had been snapped up by Trudeau's Dry Cleaners, a firm that wished to expand and were interested in the lot but not the house that sat there. (The three cardinal rules of a retail business: location, location, and location. The lot was on a busy street, and sat on the right-hand side of the road when *going* to work). The house was scheduled for demolition, and at that time any unwanted building could be purchased for a dollar as long as it was moved by a certain date. I think it's still that way, and the price hasn't really changed because it's a win-win deal. The purchaser gets a cheap house, albeit used and maybe a bit shaken up after its eventual journey to a new site. The vendor eliminates his demolition costs, including the clearing away a major part of the rubble and any liability incurred in doing so.

The lot and the basement on 74th Street where the house was moved cost six hundred dollars, all told. I know this because Mother raised the issue with us often enough and I don't blame her—because it was her relatives who eventually got stiffed for the six hundred. Uncle George loaned my parents the money to move the building and buy the lot. Typically, this loan was never repaid and became yet another source of tension between my mother and father. We kids were used to it, though. The pair frequently fought, sometimes quite violently, and Mother was by far the more aggressive of the two. It's just the way it was, and we all learned to just carry on.

The new address meant a new school, Bonnie Doon, and this was where I completed my high school years. It was also the period when the sexual abuse reached its highest intensity and, in doing so, eventually took a blatant turn that by today's standards of awareness would sound incredibly bizarre. In fact, even by the standards of the fifties it must have been incredibly bizarre, but in our house it just seemed to happen, and nobody other than me seemed to notice.

The new home was at first quite crowded. There were two bedrooms upstairs, one occupied by my parents and the second shared by my two sisters and my brother, who was now nearing three. I slept in the open basement until two bedrooms were quickly built there after we moved in, one for my sisters and the second for me, despite my protests. The last thing I wanted was to once more have a room of my own. I needn't have worried on that count, however. Father had found a door for my bedroom that could be had for nothing, but it contained a large window that made any privacy impossible. In the long run, though, it didn't matter as the situation just grew odder and odder.

The auto body shop was a quick walk down the alley behind the house, and sometime during that summer of 1958 my father made the arrangements to purchase the business from his employer, John T. By then I was working there after school and on weekends, and also on school holidays. The job eventually led to me doing full paint jobs, but in the early days it involved sanding and masking cars ready for painting, plus doing the odd bit of basic bodywork. The building was quite new, but it had a hauntingly familiar washroom, right down to the Canadian

Linen Supply towel rack. In that unpainted washroom, the sexual abuse continued, just as it had been that first day at The Bump Shop.

I say that the sexual abuse continued, but I've long considered the abuse that happened to me relatively mild compared to what could have occurred, and indeed is regularly inflicted upon less fortunate children all over the world. Father indulged his urges by coercion, not by outright violence. He was also not particularly invasive physically—except for a couple of incidents that I'll reveal in a moment.

This doesn't mean I'm trying to make light of what happened. Sexual abuse in any form is an act of violence in itself. It is an outrageous invasion of body and mind. From a legal standpoint, sexual abuse is automatically listed as a violent crime, regardless of the extent of physical damage incurred. To put my use of the word "violent" in context when stating that my father was not violent, there was no physical damage, harm, or painful constraint that occurred during the period of sexual abuse. In other words, he was not a physically violent man, and the abuse I was subject to was *relatively* benign.

It was in the new body shop that Father experimented with sodomy, but this only occurred twice—probably because of a premier performance on my behalf the first time it happened. I think by then I was beginning to realize there was a limit to how far my father was willing to force his abuse upon me. He'd quickly backed off on the oral sex, and now here he was again, doing something new. As soon as penetration occurred, I let loose a good deal of yelping and squirming that was definitely not feigned, but was certainly exaggerated. Sure, the act was a shock in itself and it did hurt, but this *was* a kid who two years before had managed not to wince too badly when lashed with a bamboo cane at school, in England. I can tell you this: that caning hurt a hell of a lot more, and it was supposed to be done for my own good. On the other hand, I can also unequivocally state that the caning was a hell of a lot less degrading.

My instant reaction to the sodomy was as much from the indignity of it as anything else. It was a total affront to body and spirit. A second attempt followed only days later, accompanied by an Oscar-worthy performance from the victim, and Father never bothered again. Neither incident actually lasted very long, which indicates Father's state of excitement. Looking back, I think he probably realized, for lack of a better way of phrasing it, that he'd again passed beyond my limit, and decided not to force the issue. I believe that this incident, perhaps at first unconsciously, finally instilled the notion that I just might have a say in what was going on.

As to the less sordid details, both acts of sodomy were carried out in the garage washroom, which reeked of the now familiar canned commercial hand soap, and the sharp but not unpleasant odour of new paint. Oddly enough, a crystal clear image remains in my mind, one that is sadly amusing. It's of Father standing in grimy green shirttails in that damned washroom when it was all over, his pants around his ankles and a shrinking penis protruding from below a grubby shirt.

There is probably no sight more pathetic.

CHAPTER SIX

Back then, nearly everyone was abused to some extent ...

It might be worth a word or two at this juncture on what is probably a more prevalent form of abuse: physical abuse. Until the end of the 1960s youngsters, particularly boys, were regularly subjected at school to what we would today call physical abuse. This was especially true in England. Having been on the receiving end more times than I care to remember, I believe this may have influenced the manner in which I coped with Father's sexual abuse. Oddly enough, I think it may have helped.

The two forms of abuse, physical and sexual, have many traits in common. Both are wide-ranging in their degree, though understandably society has greater difficulty in identifying the line crossed before physical punishment becomes physical abuse. This often fuzzy boundary may differ from one nation to another and even one faith to another, even in the West. This is probably because physical punishment, in one form or another, has been an accepted mode of discipline since time began, particularly for children. Heck, even a lioness belts her cub around the ears to teach it what not to do. Nonetheless, most people would agree that an acceptable definition of physical abuse of all children will run the gamut from the overzealous disciplining of a child to the vicious beating and even torture of that same child. Everything in between is a matter of degree.

Society's attitude on this topic has also shifted, particularly when it comes to parental discipline. Over the past sixty years, the definition of physical abuse (if indeed one existed before that) has expanded considerably to include almost any form of physical hurt. And who knows where it will be in another sixty years? I raise this issue due to the paradoxical manner in which most young boys of my era were subjected to what *today*, and only today, would be classed as physical abuse. You see, the only severe physical punishment I ever received as a youngster was inflicted by the state, also known as the school system.

One of the greatest ironies of what today is considered physical abuse is that, up until the 1960s, it was regularly dished out by society (e.g., the school system or the penal system). It was euphemistically called corporal punishment ("*of the body*," from the Latin *corpus, the body*). At school, the teachers piously referred to it as "just reward for bad behaviour."

The closest my father came to physical abuse was no more than a good swat on the butt—which at the time was not a bad thing. I still feel it has its place today, though certainly more moderately applied. For example, a sharp tap on the wrist or the behind of a child is a firm, effective way of correction when he picks up a neighbour's china vase for the *second* time, after being told not to do so (provided he's no longer holding the darn thing). I'd go a step further in this area by suggesting that any adult who becomes ensnared in a coaxing debate with a three-year-old as to whether or not that vase should be left on the table has just proved which of the two is the smarter.

This leads to a curious thought that suddenly popped into my mind, even as I'm writing. Was there a parallel between my father's relatively passive approach to dishing out any sort of corporal punishment, and the manner in which he carried out the sexual abuse?

The question is mere musing, more about trying to understand my father than anything else. As mentioned before, he wasn't a violent man. He insisted and coerced, but he didn't use force, and when he pushed beyond what was, in retrospect—I'm loath to admit—a kind of tolerance level, he backed off. I guess what I'm driving at is this: it would appear that my father's basic nature also determined the manner (and degree?) in which he committed the sexual abuse. Hmmm … I suppose all that this means, once again, is that things could have been worse.

It certainly doesn't mitigate in any way the seriousness of what he did either to me or, later on, to others. Nor does it mitigate the seriousness of the crimes of any other pedophile, except perhaps in considering the severity of the sentence when found guilty. And that's not to suggest that pedophiles who aren't violent should "get off light," either, which is a topic that will be discussed later. However, it would seem clear that the extent of violence involved in any crime would be one of the criteria involved in determining the sentence.

As to the initial suggestion—that the early, relatively harsh punishment received at school might have helped me keep the sexual abuse in perspective—this is more than mere musing. The occasional thrashing I received at school might help explain why my father's sexual abuse was more or less pigeonholed, set to one side, so to speak, allowing me to get on with my life almost as if it never happened. Because in one way, by the time it started, I was already used to doing exactly that at school.

Caning was a normal part of school life for nearly all English kids back then, particularly if they attended a school for boys. Generation after generation of young males thought nothing of what today would be called beatings, other than when being hauled onto the carpet to receive one. (And believe me, we didn't think much of it then, either). In fairness, I should state that upon arriving in Canada, I found the extent of corporal punishment in the schools much less harsh than that of Britain, and less frequently applied—which came as a very nice surprise!

Being on the sharp end of a caning was a hazard to be avoided at all costs, but when it did occur, you soon put it all behind you (in more ways than one). It was a punishment, yes, and it hurt like hell, but once administered it was over and done. You shrugged and got on with life. This was exactly what I did with the sexual abuse, as well.

One of the psychological similarities between sexual and physical abuse (such as harsh corporal punishment) *may* be that the victim considers both forms of abuse an undeserved punishment. The primary difference is that corporal punishment is usually inflicted for some sort of bad behaviour, regardless of whether the punishment fits the crime. Sexual abuse, however, is inflicted on the truly innocent. Nonetheless, victims of both detest what has happened to them, and likely feel that even corporal punishment was partly, perhaps even fully, unwarranted.

This similarity may have helped me link the two forms of abuse in the following way, even if I didn't do it consciously. Once over and done with, the "punishment" of sexual abuse, just like a caning at school, was mentally tucked away on a shelf so that normal life could on. This behaviour can be paradoxically compared in another sense that sounds all too familiar: you often concealed corporal punishment inflicted at school from your parent(s), for fear of being in greater trouble (in those days, anyway); sexual "punishment" inflicted by an adult might similarly be kept hidden because you were afraid of *creating* more trouble.

There was one big difference in this area, though, and it's worthy of mention. The tougher the corporal punishment, or physical abuse, if you will, the more brag-worthy it was to your peers. Sexual abuse, on the other hand, would never, ever be mentioned to a soul, especially to your peers.

To get to the heart of it: this seemingly absurd way of reasoning results in an almost automatic silence about abuse, particularly sexual abuse, as the young mind thinks it through and decides that telling anyone will simply bring more difficulties that might prove greater than the ones inflicted. Silence, then becomes the answer.

To many kids, this kind of thinking, and logic, is natural. It is self-protective reasoning, figured out by minds far too young to understand that keeping silent actually causes further harm, not only to themselves but also to later victims. Yet what they do is perversely logical. Whether a child is physically or sexually abused, or even steals a cookie, there is a similarity—this youngster knows inside that it's wrong, regardless of who is at fault. And in knowing it is wrong, instinct then kicks in: keep it quiet in order to avoid even more problems.

If we accept the above, then that begs the question: what happened to me previously that might be considered as physical abuse harsh enough to create that kind of a mindset? A quick summary of my school years might help explain, focusing on the British education system, and attending a school that sometimes smacked (pun intended) of *Tom Brown's School Days*.

The Canadian system was benign by comparison, and I thrived in the atmosphere here (which didn't necessarily mean doing well in school). I attended classes and acted more or less like any other student, especially my peers in the bottom quartile. While the social life was wonderful, my record as a student was appalling. By standard testing I was supposed to be what they now call "gifted," but I hated schoolwork and did just enough to scrape by. This was relatively easy, because much of the material I did manage to absorb in the English grammar school system pretty well got me through until the end of grade twelve. As a result, I rarely had a run-in with my Canadian teachers, which was a welcome change.

To be quite candid, this was an enormous change. I found school in England was a cross between a classroom and a medieval dungeon, and coming to Canada was like being paroled. I spent the last three years before emigrating at Nunthorpe Grammar School, an academic prison staffed by black-gowned masters (teachers) trained by the Spanish Inquisition. And if that description sounds a trifle exaggerated, by modern standards it's not as farfetched as it might seem.

Just thinking back for a minute or two, I can recall which teacher chose which weapon, and I was walloped by most of them. A bamboo cane was the usual instrument of choice, and was probably standard issue at teacher's college. The geography master used his walking stick, which was handy for him because he needed one to prop himself up. A running shoe was the natural choice of the gym teacher. The tempered steel strop from a T-square was used in metalwork class, while a thin slat of hardwood was applied in the woodworking shop. During physics, a small bar magnet tapping the back of the head punctuated each mistake as it was read aloud to the class. The French teacher regularly threw a piece of chalk, until he nailed one student in the eye, and his face promptly turned as white as his chalk. His nickname, coincidentally, was Greasy Graham.

A small tale, literally out of school: 'Rabbi Ben' Bowden, the master teaching Latin and Scripture, had a cane but seldom used it. The young man was probably quite well-intentioned, for he was one of the mildest members of the teaching staff, and because of that, he was the master we pushed to the limit. One day he actually snapped. (Talk about *Lord of the Flies*!) He lost his temper and hauled a tall, gangly lad called Avison to the front of the class by the collar of his jacket, where he opened the top of his tall Victorian desk and shoved the lad in headfirst. I can still hear the thud as his skull struck bottom. Bowden proceeded to belt the poor lad across the shoulders and back with a large Bible until he'd vented his spleen. Then, red faced but acting as if nothing had happened, he ordered Avison back to his desk and continued with the lesson. All thirty-four of us little barbarians sat through the remainder of that class as quiet as a platoon of Terracotta soldiers.

My worst thrashing came only two days before leaving the school for good. It was as if the gods decided to take a last kick at the cat just before the poor beast moved on and found sanctuary. Someone hit a cricket ball onto the school roof during a scrub game over lunch hour, and I shinnied up the drainpipe to retrieve it. I came down square into the arms of the English master, a balding Mr. Smith, who frowned, gave a curt nod, and uttered the dreaded words, "Report to the Head, Clews. Tell him why you're there." (The headmaster of a school was nicknamed The Head, equivalent to a school principal in Canada; it's also slang for a ship's toilet, a coincidence we relished.)

Despite a multitude of offences over the prior three years, fortune had been relatively kind. I'd never visited the inside of the headmaster's study, nor faced its godlike occupant on a one to one basis. Even so, I had no reason to believe that any serious trouble lay in store. After all, it was just a ball on the roof; punishment would likely be a hundred lines, and even at that I might be away to Canada before having to turn them in. I honestly didn't think climbing onto the roof was a hanging offence, or I would have stuffed my trousers with the usual half-dozen sheets of writing paper: not thick enough to show or sound different when hit, but not too thin to stop most of the pain.

Headmaster Moore remained seated behind his desk as I meekly edged in and reported the crime. When confession ended, he leaned back in his chair and stared in silence for the longest moment, surely, in itself, a deliberate form of torture. (Delete the last two letters and you can rearrange what's left to spell "tutor"—coincidence?) Then he sighed in feigned reluctance and walked over to the corner of the room to retrieve a slender cane, a viciously thin piece of bamboo, much skinnier than those the other masters carried. Picking it up, he turned to me, flexed it like a bow, and said, "Bend over, Clews."

Huh? I was appalled! *For climbing on the roof?* Nonetheless, after a moment's hesitation, I did as I was told.

He stepped up to my backside and again there was a pause before he asked, "What form (year within the school) are you in, Clews?"

"T-third, sir."

"Right!" Three lusty lashes on my thinly clad bottom followed.

Again there was silence as I waited, trembling and, quite successfully actually, doing my damnedest not to cry. But it wasn't over.

"I hear you're leaving for Canada this week, Clews."

Obedience was so ingrained that I was still, stupidly, bent over. "Y-yes, sir."

"Well, here's one for good luck!" And the sadistic S.O.B. hauled back and put everything he had into that one last stroke.

I challenge any young lad to stand still after that. I stumbled forward, hands flying to a bottom that felt as if it was on fire, and stepped gingerly from foot to foot while tenderly rubbing my bum. Meanwhile, the Head again flexed his cane and returned it to its corner, clearly satisfied with a job well done. In fact, and I don't say this lightly, I believe the sadistic sod found the whole episode quite amusing. How else could one interpret his *bon mot*, "one for good luck"? I remember little else of what was said after that, but I believe the callous bugger had the gall to wish me all the best in my new land.

The headmaster's office was on the second floor of the old Victorian part of the school, and I limped out just glad to be free of the place. I went home, which at the time was my mother's parents' house because Father was already in Canada, and said nothing. This was standard operating procedure. If you got into trouble at school, you sure as heck didn't tell anyone at home. That would be what's now referred to as double jeopardy.

By the time I went to bed I was fairly comfortable in terms of both pain and dodging any repercussions at home. Now the most exciting part of my life was drawing near, and I was looking forward to that last day of school. There was an heroic aura about leaving for Canada at school, somewhat akin to an intrepid adventurer departing for unexplored lands. I was the only boy so far to do such a thing, and this was on my mind as I drifted off to sleep.

Then my mother called me downstairs.

"What happened at school today?" she demanded when I sleepily entered my grandparents' living room

Baffled, I looked around at my mother, my grandfather, and my grandmother, all staring at me as grimly as the proverbial reaper. *How on earth did they find out?*

It turned out that my mother had found streaks of blood on my underpants when sorting my clothes for the wash, and now my grandfather insisted on inspecting the cause. We went into the next room (thank heavens), and for the second time that day I was told to bend over, only this time down came my pyjama bottoms. My grandfather was immediately incensed, particularly when he discovered the reason for the punishment, but his wrath wasn't directed toward me. It was directed toward Mr. Moore—which struck me as incredible!

He wanted my mother and grandmother to come in and take a look, but I at least managed to fend off that embarrassment. Instead he held up a mirror and had me take a peek. I saw four purple-blue welts across my buttocks, three of them tiny, narrow ridges with broken skin across the apex with needle-thin streaks of blood. The fourth, the final stroke, was much larger, a sharp cut clear across the skin along the welt. Such was my "good luck" send-off to Canada.

My grandfather wanted to go down to the school the next day and do battle. I wouldn't have it. The embarrassment, the shame of my peers! (Sound familiar?) He told me I didn't have to go to school the next day, which would normally have been a dream come true, but on that particular day I wouldn't have missed school for the world. So, like many other wrongs deserving some form of adult redress, the event passed unremarked. Mr. Moore no doubt continued to apply similar punishment to his charges (again, sound familiar?), quite secure in the belief that he was doing the right thing (something the sexual abuser can never honestly claim, no matter how hard he pretends).

In many ways, Moore's reasoning is readily explained. He had likely been schooled the same way, and the odd thrashing certainly hadn't done him any harm, had it?

Yeah—and so it continues!

***

So it wasn't just those girls walking the halls of learning that made school in Canada such a heavenly place to be. I was only once on the wrong end of a round of Canadian corporal punishment: four across the palm with a strap. It was delivered by a grade nine teacher called Cox, who decided that asking "Why?" when he told me to do something was out of order. He probably felt the response threatened his grip on the class, and it may very well have—I never said I was an angel.

If nothing else, that "four on the paw" completed the spectrum. I'd never had the "strap" before, nor at anytime thereafter. It tingled for awhile, but certainly didn't leave a bruised and bloody strip that required hopping from one foot to the other while trying to live with the pain. And never mind what it's called today, a caning that split the skin, even in the fifties, would probably have been officially considered physical abuse of a child. At a grammar school like Nunthorpe, however, even in the unlikely event that such an incident was reported, it's doubtful any action would have been taken. Similar to cases of sexual abuse—and this also sounds all too familiar—the authorities at the time, whether the law or the church, would have probably filed the complaint in a cubbyhole.

As to the punishment itself, at the time it was no big deal. Now I'm older, however, I find it difficult to understand how a grown, educated man could actually do that—never mind to me, but to kids as young as eleven years old.

Returning to why I raise this issue: did this earlier treatment help me cope with the sexual abuse that occurred soon after? At bare minimum I think it assisted in keeping matters in perspective, namely placing the sexual abuse where I felt it belonged: in exactly the same place as the thrashings at school. Okay, so it happened. It's over for now at least, so forget about it and hope it doesn't happen again. But if it does, well, forget about that too and hope it doesn't happen again. And if it does, well ...

In that manner, both kinds of abuse may be similar. And the saddest part is that in either type, the victims find it more convenient to remain silent.

***

There may have been one further factor that helped deal with Father's abuse, and I'm not particularly proud of it: attitude. I was a 'self-confident' brat, a description that regularly appeared on my report cards (*sans* the word brat). This was probably because it was the only honest comment available to my teachers that might vaguely sound positive. (It is, in fact, a frustrated teacher's way of saying, "He's a cocky little bastard.")

Such an attitude generally produces a kid who is convinced that the punishment dished out at school, for example, is never his fault. Episodes such as the cricket ball on the roof certainly helped keep that way of thinking alive. The end result was that the punishment at school was, in my mind, rarely my fault—or, even if it was, it certainly was never appropriate for the crime. It was always "the teacher's fault" or, if it wasn't, then "I didn't deserve what I got."

Later, when Father's sexual abuse started, this attitude likely conditioned me to accept and deal with events that were truly not my fault—and, like the caning, put them in a pigeonhole to be forgotten. I don't know if that's true or not, but I do know that the sexual abuse didn't *seem* to affect me that much, at the time. Not in any noticeable manner, anyway ... I think. If this is true, it's ironic that those personal traits that were really character flaws could have helped deal with the sexual abuse. It's a heck of a thought.

I did manage to bumble along through grades ten, eleven, and twelve, and somehow gained a Senior Matriculation Certificate with grades so close to failing you could hear them grate as they scraped over the bar. These marks were phenomenally below my statistical (tested) capability, a situation that was ever the bane of my teachers—the ones who cared, anyway. I mention this only to show that the sexual abuse from my father was never the cause of a dismal record at school. My grades had fallen miserably long before that began.

But they were not always bad. Before that disastrous entry into Nunthorpe Grammar School, I had been the star student at primary school, and no doubt coddled accordingly. Maybe it was the wrong thing to do, but the headmistress let me take the eleven-plus test when I was only ten, and I arrived at Nunthorpe a year early. I handled it badly, of that there is no doubt. On our arrival in Canada, my mother lied to the school authorities when enrolling me, telling them we had left England before receiving my report card. She had it—the teachers in England went out of their way to get it ready for her—but it was too embarrassing to show. They probably would have sent me back to grade three.

Even so, a child's mind is a sponge that always absorbs something, no matter where it wanders. A good deal of that grammar school knowledge was regurgitated during my four Canadian school years, and it somehow managed to filter through the daydreaming and doodling that filled most of my classroom time when coasting to the end of grade twelve. Some of the reasons for my near failure were likely valid, but it didn't matter, because someone up there seemed to be looking out for me.

CHAPTER SEVEN

The stakes are raised, but the dealer folds ...

The end of the abuse was drawing near, but the most blatant and unbelievable twist of the two and a half years had yet to occur. It began one day when nobody else was at home. I had returned from working at the body shop, leaving Father to paint whatever vehicle I'd finished preparing. It was probably only a single fender or a door panel, because it didn't take long before he, too, came home.

In the meantime, I'd fallen into a nice hot bath and was cleaning myself of the paint dust and whatever other dirt that had managed to glom to the skin during the day. I was enjoying the steaming, sudsy water in the only tub in the house when the door handle turned. Nothing new there, everyone tried the handle when the door was closed, testing to see if the bathroom was unoccupied. But the door jiggled again, rattling against the small bolt that served as a lock. Then came the all too familiar knocking.

"Graham?"

Who the hell else would be in here? "I'll be out in a minute."

"Let me in."

I quickly got out of the bath and started towelling myself, kicking at the dirty pile of clothes to sort them out. "I said I'll be finished in a minute."

"I need the bathroom now."

This verbal back and forth went on for maybe another half-minute, until finally Father snapped, "I said open the door!"

Fifteen years of obedience again kicked in, and I meekly opened the door. There's no point in going into what happened next, other than to say it was the same old thing, only this time we were both naked in a hot, steamy bathroom. Father seemed to have discovered a new venue, and a new lease on an old theme. And while this particular incident was not particularly surprising because the house was otherwise empty, what happened in the months that followed certainly was. In fact, it was incredible. The next time it happened, Mother was at home with the kids, watching television in the front room.

***

Since I was going to school during the day, evenings and weekends made up my work schedule, other than during school holidays, when the work was full-time. I was the only employee who consistently worked after regular hours and, for that matter, the only employee who worked without getting a paycheque. Remuneration came in the form of pocket money, and it had to be asked for: a few dollars dished out on the weekend, for a movie or the like. This was natural in those days, and there were no complaints or sense of injustice. After all, I was only fifteen and this was the fifties—what was I going to spend it on, anyway? Certainly not an iPod or a cell phone, and as for clothes, what was wrong with a pair of jeans and a flannel shirt, the latter on sale at Woodward's on $1.49 Day.

So I worked, and I didn't really mind it at all; and when things are busy in the world of small business, long hours are part of the deal. I have worked them when necessary, all my life. You either cater to your customers' needs, or you go out of business. My father did manage to instill in me a good, solid work ethic, and for that I'm grateful. It was his darker life lessons I could have cheerfully done without. And this new twist in applying them became predictable, based entirely on what remained to be done at the body shop when the shift ended.

The painting of an entire car was Father's job, though by then I was learning to do the smaller stuff. Painting was almost always done at the end of the day or in the evening, when the chance of dust being sucked from the shop to settle on the newly applied paint in the paint booth was reduced to almost nil. When there were no cars ready to paint, we'd both go home together.

At the end of a work day, grimed up and badly in need of a wash, a soak in the warm tub was second heaven, one to be anticipated despite even the normal interruptions: "Hey, come on, get out of there—I gotta *go!*" If I'd left Father with maybe just a fender or a hood in need of paint, I would have a quick dip and get out fast. If he had a complete paint job to do, the bathroom was good for at least an hour—though half an hour was usually the limit before someone else was banging on the door. If we arrived home together, the bathroom became the last place to relax.

I tried a new strategy to avoid Father, which led to the final irony in his new, brazen choice of venue. When we did arrive home together I would skip the bath and take my shirt off, choosing only to wash my hands and face with the door wide open. Afterward I'd go downstairs to change into clean jeans, then come back upstairs to watch television or doodle with my homework. As with any change in routine, however, this only worked a time or two before Father caught on and blatantly changed the format. This time his words were meant for Mother, not me: "Don't be so lazy, Graham. You need a darn good bath before you go to school tomorrow."

And as I disappeared into the bathroom, he followed up with, "Leave the door unlocked, I need a bath too. And don't drain the water."

I submissively followed instructions and ran a tub. To argue the issue in front of Mother would, in my mind, have only called attention to what was really going on. Not only that, talking back to my father would have been out of character, even if I'd plucked up the courage to do so. Either way, she would surely want to know what the problem was, and for sure I didn't dare tell her. And so, in this manner I continued protecting Father from being discovered, by hiding the truth from my mother. It never occurred to me that she might have known, or at least suspected, and simply chose to bury whatever thoughts were running through her mind.

That first time we arrived home together I hopped in the tub and quickly washed, but within a minute or two he was in there and it was a case of here we go again, only this time Mother was now in the next room. How on earth did he manage to summon up the barefaced gall to do this? Had he grown so confident, and Mother so naïve—or willfully oblivious—that he just assumed his conduct would be accepted? The answer to both questions can probably be found in the behaviour of all those who do exactly what they want to do and continually get their way. They simply keep pushing the limit until everything blows up.

Only nothing blew up.

This "double bathing" didn't happen that often, mind you. In all, there were probably less than a dozen such incidents and that's just a guess, because I sure didn't keep count. I would lock the door even though told not to, only to again hear the jiggle of the lock and the familiar soft rap of knuckles on wood. I would finally give in, though for the first time I was now feeling real anger, in part due to the openness of it all and the resulting stress, and also because I was growing older and finally developing a backbone. Even so, as the whispers grew more garrulous, I eventually obeyed and opened the door—because I didn't want anyone, particularly Mother, to think that something untoward was going on! She seemed to accept this behaviour as the norm though, and in a way I suppose my own cover-up may have been partly responsible for her being able to rationalize what was going on.

The bathroom venue continued quite sporadically for several months. During that time my mother did ask once—the question seemed more curious than anything else—why Father took his bath with me still in the room. I mumbled something about men taking baths together—after all, look at the showers at school, which was true. The boys all stripped down and showered together, as did the girls, presumably. Lame as the reason was, incredibly, Mother accepted it—or again, "rationalized" might be a better word. As to my part in effectively helping Father, by then the "big secret" had simply become a regular part of my life that I kept hidden from everyone. To reveal it would have led to such enormous consequences, both real and imagined, none of which I was prepared to set in motion. By then it just seemed easier to live with what was going on.

Yet finally ending the abuse, at least as far as it directly affected me, proved surprisingly simple.

Even though my life seemed to be going quite well outside of the home, the tension with Father continued to build as, phenomenally late in life, I gradually started to become my own person. I was probably approaching sixteen when, with the noise of the television in the living room carrying into the bathroom, I once more heard the dreaded knocking. The demand came in a low voice, as usual, and like so many times before, the *'I'll just ignore the knocking'* charade played out. Perhaps a bit of the "I'll be out in a minute" routine followed. Quite frankly, I have no memory of the preliminary verbal sparring and it no longer matters. What did happen was, for lack of a better way of putting it, I lost my temper—or composure. Where it came from I still don't know, but something just gave way inside. In desperation, I yelled at the door, "Just bugger off!"

As soon as the words were out, I was horrified. A long, deadly silence followed. A silence that stretched, and stretched, and stretched and I wondered what sort of storm I'd created on the other side of the door. Then, as the minutes passed, I slowly realized that Father had gone away. I lingered in the bathroom for ages wondering what to do, before even thinking about coming out. Yet when I did, there was nothing. Father had simply gone away!

And that was the end of it. In the words of that well-known Canadian home handyman: it was just that easy! Oh, Father was far from friendly when we finally met face to face, but he wasn't openly enraged. In fact, it was as if nothing of consequence had happened. The only apparent change, ironically, was that now Father seemed to be the cold, sullen one, not me—both at home and at work.

The days, then the weeks, were like waiting for the sword of Damocles to fall. This had truly been my first act of open defiance with Father on anything, and retribution surely waited in the wings. And even if it did not, there was still the dreaded expectation of the next knocking at the bathroom door, or the invasion of the washroom at work—but neither happened.

The sexual abuse was over, and for good.

It never entered my mind that maybe his perverted taste for children had no further need of his oldest son.

CHAPTER EIGHT

The lost art of careful career planning, and a further shock …

Grade twelve graduation was supposed to be in 1960, about a year and half after the abuse stopped. When the final term finished I was still at loose ends, unsure what to do as I waited for what were undoubtedly bad marks on the final exams. Like a lot of things in my life, however, matters ultimately seemed to resolve themselves. What ensued that summer turned out to be a comedy of errors that literally changed the entire direction of my life, and all for the better. I still shake my head at the way everything fell into place, for the bumbling mistakes of the next twelve months might have been orchestrated by a mischievous but very benign gang of hobgoblins. Or, more simply put, someone, somewhere, was looking after me, and had a dark sense of humour.

There was no money available for further education and even if had there been, I hadn't the faintest idea what I wanted to be. Nor did I have the marks to do it, anyway. I still had a full-time summer job in the auto body shop, however, at the usual buck an hour. It seemed like a good option while biding time. This meant there were usually a few dollars in my pocket, but only if there was enough money in Crown Auto Body's bank account to issue a paycheque. More often than not, I got a few bucks on the weekend for a date, rather than the forty or fifty dollars earned that week, but that's just the way it was. Besides, if I had been paid, a third of it would have gone on room and board anyway.

(As an accountant, I feel obliged to pause and offer a comment on that buck an hour rate of pay. Oddly enough, it was not a bad wage for a seventeen-year-old. This, or maybe $1.10 at the most, was the rate for an unskilled, low-end young labourer who was willing to take any kind of job. Surprisingly enough, the journeyman auto body worker was only making about $2.25 to $2.40 an hour. That's 125–135 percent more than the unskilled youth working in the shop, in an economy that was starting to boom. Today, however, a skilled tradesman will make 300–400 percent more than the unskilled youth—and the professions have widened the gap much, much further—and that's without their obscene tax advantages. The difference has created a far wider 'class' disparity in earnings over the years that should not exist..

This all contributes to the growing gap in remuneration between rich and poor that you hear about today. A gap that is dragging heavily on the economy and the welfare system—and that's without taking into account the indecent proliferation of seven- and eight-figure annual paycheques being picked up by the easy-dollar-salary/bonus-greedy nouveau riche. Nonetheless, the answer to the problem lies not in cutting the top end, though some of the blatant high-rolling stuff does need to be choked off—$47,000,000 a year for Judge Judy, for God's sake—it's the lower end that requires an enormous boost. Not only because the people in that lower end can then catch up and start contributing more to the economy. They need it to be able to survive with dignity.)

Not long after school ended, the results of my final exams arrived and the fickle finger of fate, for better or for worse, appeared to take all choice of career planning out of my hands. The marks were an utter disaster. Any other papers buried within the thick envelope were carelessly tossed aside as I read the one that listed the marks, for there it was in black and white: *Chemistry 30: 46%*. One of the core subjects, and I'd missed it! Failure!

But then ... so what?

And that comment was not sour grapes. It just didn't seem like a big deal at the time. I'd simply move to plan B—as soon as it came to mind. This "who cares" attitude stemmed from—well, it stemmed from my normal, everyday attitude back then. I was only seventeen and, other than the classes and the homework, school was pretty good. I had my own car by then, a 1953 Meteor two-door sedan that I'd bought as a wreck for $262.50. I'd fixed it up in the shop, brand new paint included, and it looked pretty sharp. And with the abuse now over for more than a year and a half, life was going great. So, I simply continued at school for another year, attending in the morning to boost my marks, and working at the auto body shop in the afternoon and on weekends. To what end, though, I still had no idea.

Another side story: I managed to accumulate the funds to pay for the car during the summer of 1959. That was the only time I ever got a regular paycheque from Crown Auto Body. I worked an average of fifty hours a week over the school holidays, which resulted in about fifty dollars for each of the eight weeks. The reason for the regular pay was that my grandmother came over that year for the entire summer, and Father dared *not* pay me while she was there. Mind you, after she returned to England, Father hit me up for the hundred and twenty bucks that remained after buying the car and fixing it up, because he wanted a small rowboat, supposedly for fishing. He never paid it back. On the other hand, I did get to use the boat.

On the surface of it, returning to school was one of the dumbest, most ill-informed moves I ever made in my life. It must have coaxed an exasperated sigh from the Three Goddesses of Fate, and then perhaps a small smile, for it also proved to be the most fortunate decision of my life. Once in a while, being a bit of a dummy *may* be an asset; and being a careless, neglectful, lazy, ill-informed dummy can sometimes work out even better. You see, I had never paid any attention to the paperwork that came with the marks. I should have, but thank goodness I didn't. Not for another seven months, anyway. I had actually passed grade twelve the first time!

One of the documents I'd tossed aside in the mad rush for the marks was a Senior Matriculation Certificate. Yet, had I taken the time to look through the discarded pile and find that important piece of paper, I would have been back at square one: what am I going to do with the rest of my life, with no funds or everyday savvy to compensate? The prospects were not great.

So, not looking for the certificate was the dummy part. As to the Fates smiling, they must have chuckled several times during that second, otherwise pointless year of grade twelve.

The first time would have been when Marie Harrison showed up in grade ten, and in October we began dating. We were married in 1963, and are still married—and to each other, too.

Another "chuckle" was surely warranted the following February, when I was summarily ejected from Latin class for sloth and misbehaviour. This forced a meeting with the school counsellor, the first such encounter in over three and a half years of schooling. Miss Scott was an older, severe-looking lady with grey hair and twinkling blue-grey eyes. I think she actually liked me—really. She was relaxed and chatty, shuffling through my file as we spoke. Then, out of the blue, her expression grew puzzled and she asked, "Why are you here, anyway, Graham?"

I shrugged, deciding the question was general rather than the ejection from Latin class. "I'm trying to get my senior matriculation."

"You already have it."

"No, Miss Scott, I failed chemistry."

Frowning, she again studied the file, then she nodded as if it was suddenly all clear. "I see you passed physics, though, and that gives you one science, which in your case is all that's required. You can substitute one of your two foreign language credits for the other science."

"But my average—"

"A sixty percent average is required for a matriculation diploma, *Mister* Clews!" The emphasis fell very hard on the word "Mister" as Miss Scott shook her head as if in despair. "When one of the foreign languages is substituted and the chemistry dropped, you have achieved a sixty and one half percent average as your final mark."

"Oh. I see ..."

The logical choice was to then move to plan C, a notion that had been percolating, on and off, for the best part of a year. There was no further point in going back to school every morning for the two classes that now remained, and I hated chemistry anyway, so the next day I was off to the RCMP to join up. Fortunately, the officer who staffed the recruiting desk that morning seemed to be even thicker than I was. The conversation, which would have been chuckle number three, went like this:

"I'd like to fill out an application to join up, sir."

"What are you doing now, son?"

"Well, I was going to school, but I quit yesterday."

"Sorry, we don't accept applications from anyone who is quitting school to join."

"But I've already passed grade twelve. Here's my certificate."

I produced the now wrinkled document that I'd managed to unearth from the hash of papers discarded seven months before, and for the longest time it was ponderously examined. The recruiting officer frowned and for a moment appeared hesitant, but he wanted to be sure. "You said you were still going to school."

"Not really. I was, but I—"

"But you did quit, though, and come in here to apply?"

"I suppose, but that was yesterday. Besides, I have passed grade twelve, honest. Look, I've got my matric certificate right there, and—"

You could see the man's mind ticking over, the cogs slowly turning until they came back to rule number one (it doesn't matter what department of the civil service you are dealing with, it always comes back to the applicable rule number one, which is unbreakable). "Sorry, son, I'm not taking an application."

"*Aaaagh!*"

The Fates' fourth and final chuckle would have been late in May, when that second, now seemingly pointless school year had almost drawn to a close. The end of the month found me finishing my second shift in grade twelve with hardly any improvement in the marks, though as it had turned out, that didn't matter. I still had no idea what to do.

One Saturday night I found myself alone with a friend called Kelly at his parents' home, along with a bootlegged bottle of rye and his Mum and Dad away for the weekend. Alas, the rye was all we had for company, which was just as well, and even that didn't last long. Neither of us were experienced drinkers. We chugged a full bottle down in three drinks each, straight up. We drank it that way because watered down, the stuff tasted even worse. And there was no mix because, with less than fifty cents remaining between us, a pack of Export Plain had trumped a bottle of Canada Dry.

During our conversation, which by that time wasn't particularly lucid, the topic of careers came up, because in another month we'd both be finished school. I mentioned that I had no idea what I was going to do, but maybe the RCMP was an option—though there was now some doubt about that, because Marie and I had become a firm item. (In those days the only thing that got hitched in the RCMP was a horse; a recruit couldn't get married in the first five years of service). Kelly then informed me that he was moving to Stettler to article as a chartered accountant. I actually had to ask him what a chartered accountant was.

Kelly, quite innocently, lied. He told me it was the second highest paid profession in Canada, which wasn't true—but it was close enough to the mark to be too good to be true. The courses were set through the Canadian Institute of Chartered Accountants, and administered through Queens University in Toronto. A candidate didn't have to attend classes full time. Instead, he articled for five years while taking the course (an on-the-job training option phased out in 1971). And—this was the part that seemed way too good to be true—the accounting firm to which the candidate was articled actually paid a salary, starting at the princely sum of one hundred and forty dollars a month.

Before the night was over we found an advertisement in the *Edmonton Journal* (wasn't that how we arrived in Edmonton to begin with?), and the following Monday I phoned for an interview. Kelly offered a small piece of advice to send me on my way, a lie which I blithely repeated to a Mr. Gerry Robinson, CA, a wonderful man who has long passed to the other side. Deadpan, I told him, "I've been thinking of articling to become a chartered accountant since grade ten, sir."

Fortunately, the latest marks from high school were not yet out, and even more fortunate, Gerry Robinson's firm was not particularly interested in them. Christenson, Morrison & Co. was quite a progressive accounting firm that subjected their screened applicants to a barrage of tests before offering a position. Had they not been so progressive, those terrible high school marks would have left me standing outside the front door devoid of all hope, and missing out on what has proven to be a very satisfying career.

So how did I manage? The weak-sounding account on the previous pages of knuckling under to Father, along with my slipshod manner of meandering through life, would point to a youngster who wasn't particularly bright. And not being particularly bright was partly true, but that's a lot different from being smart. The narrative so far might also indicate a lad who was passive and not too willing to stand up for himself. Nothing could be further from the truth. Academically lazy, yes; an inattentive daydreamer, certainly; bored and frequently indolent, I suppose; and as dumb as a sack of hammers when it came to being focused, what can I say?

But as for not standing up for myself, well, oddly enough, that only seemed to be a problem when confronting my father. It was as if knuckling under to him was built into my genes, and this was not just applicable to the sexual abuse. I don't know why, but until that frustrated outburst from inside the bathroom, I never could stand up to my father. Everywhere else, however, I just plowed on, usually doing exactly what I wanted to do, without being particularly sensitive to what anyone else thought—which, obviously, wasn't at all a very good way to behave, either.

So that was the situation as I left school: apparently not too bright, and not particularly brave, either, at least at home. So how did a teenager so oblivious and seemingly weak-willed manage to get hired, and then pass one of the toughest courses of the times? (Out of forty-six students enrolled in the five year program in 1961, only nine of us passed within the minimum possible five year period).

To begin with, I got very quickly tuned in by joining the real world. When you are working for private enterprise, where profitability is key and bankruptcy is the only other option, you either perform or you are fired. (I did get fired that first year, but Gerry, may the angels bless him wherever he is, relented and I hung on and eventually did well). And as to how I managed to get hired in the first place with such a dismal academic background, well that proved to be the easiest part.

My sole career weapon in an otherwise barren arsenal was the ability to score ectremely high on intelligence tests, and the accounting firm took this at face value. Even so, it still took me several years to understand that this alone was not good enough. I used to baffle my teachers by not living up to expectations. I consistently performed near the bottom of the class, once finished primary school. It wasn't until my early twenties that my lazy, flaccid brain finally understood the basics: in order to do well you have to pay attention and work, the more so if you have absolutely no interest in the task to begin with (such as the basic auditing courses of the CA curriculum). The problem in my dismal school years was not accepting that in order to learn you must at least read the material, and listen to what was being said!

As for my weak will, by the end of high school this had resolved itself. At home, it was as if Father and I had reached an understanding. The abuse part was over, and as long as I put in the hours at the body shop, even though still in school I could do as I wanted. And I did, with a surprising amount of freedom.

Saturday night I would hop in my car after work, and maybe not come home until after school on Monday. In short, almost complete freedom at sixteen. The only time I pushed Father too hard was when he told me to paint a complete car one Sunday, a day when a few of us had been planning on going to the lake. He had plans for the same day. Thoroughly annoyed, I took off Saturday night for the rest of the weekend, and went straight to school Monday morning without ever going home. Father went to school too, showing up at the classroom door during the first period. He didn't tell me to come home, he just demanded my car keys. *My* car, the one I'd paid for, was registered in Father's name!

By the end of that second year in grade twelve, I would have been hard put to say why I'd ever given in to Father's sexual abuse in the first place. Part of the answer might be found in a quote by Lenin: "Give me four years to teach the children and the seed I have sown will never be uprooted." Father had me for thirteen years. So take Lenin's adage and apply it to parents who teach their kids to blindly obey, plus a school system that thrashes the same message into their backsides, then such a closed, controlling environment is damned intimidating. It takes an awful lot of grit to resort to open defiance after living under years of authoritarian discipline. Outside that environment, however, a youngster will often become just as aggressive as anyone else, perhaps even more so, in order to compensate. That certainly seemed to be the case with me.

***

Marie and I were married in June of 1963, and we both moved out of our parents' houses into a basement suite in South Edmonton. She had found a job at city hall in the utilities department, and I had bumpily completed the second of the required five years of articles in order to become a CA. But back at my former home, there was still my younger brother Steve. I knew trouble would likely arise there one day but I had yet to give any serious thought as to what to do about it. After all, Steve was still only nine years old. My problems with Father had not started until I was thirteen, and a few years still remained before Steve reached that age. Looking at that comment, it's hard to believe its stupidity, but at the time it seemed only logical: father was obviously homosexual, and Steve was safe for at least another couple of years, maybe even as many as four.

As for Father being a pedophile, the word wasn't even in my vocabulary, nor would it be for some years. It wasn't an issue that was talked about in the fifties and for some time after, so something you've never even heard of just doesn't exist. If someone had asked what the word meant, I would have probably reverted to my half-baked Latin: *pedes*, "of the feet". Then upon discovering that the last half, *phile*, was from the Greek for "a love of", I'd have figured it meant someone who likes to walk.

The root of the word pedophile is actually primarily Latin, but probably should be spelled *paedophile* (it is spelled that way in Britain) because *paedos* is the Roman word for children. And while *Philo* is from the Greek, the meaning "a love of" is not used in a sexual sense. It is more of an adherent fixation, such as "I love those Edmonton Oilers" (though the choice of the Oilers must clearly have its roots in the German *Masochismus*). Nonetheless, the American form, *pedophile*, spelled without an "a," has generally been adopted in Canada. The more accurate form would be *paederast*, which is the original British term used to describe someone who has sexual intercourse with boys. This has been extended by common usage to include girls as well, all of which shows that even the word "pedophile" has in itself become messed with over the years.

These definitions do not matter to a sexually abused child though, or a teenage immigrant. In fact, they can be confusing. Sometime after the abuse began, my own flawed logic about what was happening crystallized as mentioned above, and I concluded that Father was homosexual. Not that I was aware of that particular name either. As I grew older, I learned from my new Canadian buddies that there existed men who liked men and they were called "queers." This explanation seemed to readily explain away Father, and so the notion that any adult would have a perverse sexual interest in children never crossed my thirteen-year-old mind. Such an idea would have actually been beyond my understanding. As to concluding he was 'queer' and nothing more, that line of thinking was additionally reinforced by Father's earlier visits to the baths in that seedier part of the city called 95th Street.

Logically, then, if my father happened to take advantage of whoever was handy, it followed that only Steve was at risk from his attentions. I knew something had to be done one day, but as yet I didn't know when or how to broach the problem. It would, as far as I could see, mean waiting until he was at least old enough to understand, and I'd set the age as being around his twelfth birthday. I knew this would also mean a major confrontation with my father, and it would have to be one that resulted in some form of a clear understanding as to his future behaviour. The concern over this, even as I approached twenty-one years of age, was still something I dreaded. It was, however, something I felt could be resolved, even if it took the threat of revealing all if he didn't start behaving.

And yes, I know. Once again, how simple—no, stupid—could a person be?

I was about to find out.

The shocking disclosure came during our first year of marriage, when Marie and I were visiting my parents. An argument erupted between Father and Mother, which was not an uncommon event. This particular conflict occurred not long after Father had gone bankrupt for the second time and Mother's complaints, understandably enough, were the usual. There was not enough money, he was never at home, and he should put the family first. Going the other way, the sole positive note was that, since the close of the shop, Father had abandoned the auto body trade and was working on acquiring a pressure welding ticket. He had found a pretty good job with a decent paycheque, so God knows where the money was now going.

My oldest sister was there as the argument began, also not uncommon. All four kids regularly bore witness to our parents' scraps. Margaret was coming up on seventeen at the time. Oddly enough, for she usually stayed out of things, my sister quickly became embroiled in the fray, taking Mother's side. All three of them said some pretty down and dirty things, with my sister's words cutting a deep furrow.

Later, when it was over, the two of us met in the hallway and I suggested that there was no point in getting upset and shouting names at Father, after all, both Mum and Dad were as bad as each other when it came to the continuous fighting.

Her eyes instantly grew moist and she snapped back, "You don't know!"

The words caused an instant chill. "I don't know what?"

And it all tumbled out in a torrent of tears. She'd been twelve at the very most when he'd first "put his thing in me," as she tearfully phrased it. And, as it had happened with me, the abuse had lasted two to three years.

I was horrified, instantly and literally feeling ill, as if everything were whooshing around inside. And the sense of guilt was immediate.

CHAPTER NINE

My sister Margaret, who she was and now is …

Physically, Margaret would be called petite. She is slender, small boned, and stands about five foot two—but she does not have eyes of blue, they are hazel, inherited from her mother's side. She has always been quite attractive, even today (for her age) as she's into the third year of her old age pension. But I doubt if her physical appeal had anything to do with the sexual abuse that our father inflicted upon her. The fact that she was conveniently there, and that he happened to be a pedophile, were doubtless sufficient reasons to select her as a victim. This, and the fact that as his daughter, she was a far safer target than a stranger.

Margaret now lives on the west coast. When I spoke to her on the subject of Father and about writing this account, she felt that it was a good thing. More than that, she volunteered further information, some of which came as quite a shock. It had to do with what happened to others outside the family, events she discovered from various discussions with friends much later in life, following Father's conviction. (I suspect that once he had been jailed, people felt more willing to talk. There is probably a lesson to be found in this.) So it wasn't just Margaret's own experience of Father that sat heavy on her mind as we discussed this book, there were the experiences of others.

Margaret is not quite sure when the sexual abuse began, but it was at a younger age than it began with me. Possibly as early as ten, more likely around eleven, but it would have been on turning twelve at the very latest. Timing is one of the few things she's vague about, but my guess is the first abuse occurred before she turned twelve. That makes her pretty damned young and awfully damned small, without mentioning weak and vulnerable. It's hard to imagine. In fact, it's more than that. Just the thought that it did happen to any kid that age is both revolting and infuriating, fostering an anger that for many would have no bounds. And yet, it happens to children far younger all over the world, and the numbers are beyond belief.

The memories Margaret has are not as precise and crystal clear as my own. Perhaps they are blurred for a reason, subconscious or otherwise. Or maybe they are there, buried, and she just doesn't want to go digging for them. If so, I know to some small extent how she feels, because the nitty-gritty details are far too private to repeat, nor is it necessary to do so unless such delving is of therapeutic value. Certain key events are quite clear in her mind, however—two in particular.

The first time it occurred. This took place when she climbed into her parents' bed one morning, something that most of us have routinely done from the time we were toddlers. Only this time it happened when Father was alone and, as my sister so poignantly and painfully expressed what happened, "he put his thing in me." A second incident that is also clear in her mind: Father took her for a ride in the same damned boat I loaned the money for, on one of the lakes that are within an easy drive of Edmonton. The boat put into a small island in the lake, and after that—well, that's all that needs to be said.

These facts she volunteered. There were certainly other incidents, but I didn't ask, nor will I ever. I don't want to know, though if she wants to talk, I'll listen. We have discussed other details of our family history quite a bit when we are together, and a good deal of the talk—well, it's not happy talk. Of course there were many good times too and we remember them as well, but talking about them, more often than not, merely serves to steer the conversation toward more sombre times. The talk is rarely about the sexual abuse however, but more about life in general. Quite frankly, I think that once in a while we just like to sit down and bitch about our upbringing. Between us, the topic of sexual abuse has remained fairly dormant over the years, other than on rare occasions such as the writing of this book. Neither of us particularly wants to rehash what took place in the course of conversation. That part of the past is distasteful, of no interest, and there's little more to be said.

Any family discussion is as likely to centre upon Mother just as much as it does on Father. Perhaps this is because we both knew Father for exactly what he was: an open book with few white pages, a bunch more smudged with grey, and a whole slew of black pages—far more than are usually found in biographies. Even at that, as older adults, we also know what he was in terms of definition, which doesn't necessarily help. Clinically Father was a sick man with a recognized mental condition who callously chose never to even try to curb his hurtful tendencies. In everyday talk, he was a sex pervert who preyed on kids. He was also our father.

Mother was also an open book, but by comparison, there were enough unseen pages stuck together to leave us wondering what they contained. Margaret's questions here are mainly the same as mine. What was Mother thinking about, when all this was going on? How could she have been so dense—though was she, really? Was Father's behaviour, which would surely have been transparent to anyone else, something that she conveniently chose to ignore, or did she willfully deny it? Or did she find the consequences of dealing with Father's behaviour just too much to handle, financially and otherwise, and simply allowed the kids to become sacrificial lambs? And then, just maybe—and one hesitates to say this about one's parent, because it's not kind—was she simply as thick as the proverbial plank and did not really understand what was going on? Hmm...

Bearing the above in mind, Margaret does hold Mother at least partially responsible for the abuse, not for what initially happened to her, but because it continued to happen. She has good cause to think this way, because it's likely true, as I'll discuss later. Regardless of whether or not it was, however, Margaret grew up feeling that she was severely let down—perhaps betrayed is a better word—not by one parent, but by both. Father for the abuse he inflicted, and Mother for her willful ignorance.

Her seeming indifference, perhaps as much as Father's abuse, led Margaret to consult a psychiatrist when she was in her late twenties. This was about the time she finally told Mother what had been happening. It was a stressful period, and the psychiatrist's advice helped. Later, when she figured it was needed, she also took psychological counselling. She found this invaluable, particularly from one young woman who helped her through some very difficult times. In other words, she was having difficulties with all this and sought help, which proved to be useful.

While her father was no doubt the primary cause, Margaret was having just as many problems dealing with her mother's seemingly negligent behaviour while the abuse was happening. This generated feelings of abandonment and betrayal, dark feelings that paralleled the sexual abuse itself. To offer an analogy, there might be someone you know well and are supposed to adore and trust, and he is beating you half to death. Meanwhile, someone else who you also love and could help stop this, simply stands by watching and does nothing. Who has failed you more? Who deserves more of your anger?

With the help she sought, Margaret was able to live with the fallout and, like me, kept the dark side of her life to herself. She never had difficulty making friends, so she managed to at least live with what had happened. She graduated from high school with a good deal of hard work, because under the circumstances, learning would surely have been a chore. Her record at school was good, not spectacular perhaps, but far better than mine. Part of the reason this was possible might be due to that fact that she had always been an obedient, well-behaved youngster. Ironically, these traits may also have helped Father maintain the status quo within the family while he was abusing her. Quite possibly good behaviour in a child, generally speaking, might mean that the child does exactly as told, even when instructed by a pedophile.

The sexual abuse did affect Margaret quite a bit, as shown by her visits to a psychiatrist and several psychologists later in life. This has been a point of discussion and she says the therapy helped tremendously, but as for any overt effects that remained, even she will admit that it is difficult to say what, if any, there are. Speculating on such matters is no more than a pointless exercise, because none of us will ever know how things might have turned out if significant events in our lives never happened. Many of the "different" paths Margaret took later in life, for instance, have also been taken by others who have not been abused. And some of those paths she took are often admired by others, such as her world travel. Bearing this in mind, the following few words are simply observations, written with what might best be described as my sister's forbearance.

If Margaret had a single foible that could be laid at the door of her father's sexual abuse, it was that until late middle age she was unable to establish a good, solid relationship with a member of the opposite sex. Difficulty in attaining a stable relationship is quite common with sexually abused children, particularly girls. There were boyfriends in my sister's life, certainly, and a fairly brief marriage toward the end of her twenties that remained childless, but nothing seemed stable. That doesn't mean that women who were not abused don't have the similar problems; it's just that the odds of failed relationships are statistically higher among women who have been sexually abused as children. To this extent, Margaret fits the profile.

Margaret had lots of female friends over the years and still does, but it wasn't until later in life that she managed to settle down after meeting her present husband. Perhaps more than coincidentally, Al is a man within the same profession (teaching), and a person she gradually grew to know while they worked together as peers. In other words, it wasn't something she rushed into, and perhaps this helped. (It also helps that Al has the patience of a saint—but that's something that many a brother would likely say about the man who married his sister.)

There is another trait that might be attributed to the abuse, but as I mentioned before, we will never know for sure. By that, I mean: would we still have all those little quirks we developed along life's path, regardless of how we were raised?

Margaret has always felt a need for attention, though she doesn't openly demand it. To be more specific, she seems to have a need to be well regarded, though not in the "hail fellow, well-met, look how successful I am" manner our father yearned for. With Margaret it shows up more as "love me for who I am because I do need to be reassured". This manifests itself in several mannerisms, and as an example I'll cite the one I notice most often—and perhaps only then because I'm her brother, who sees it as her need for attention.

Margaret doesn't just order a meal in a restaurant, she almost always ponders aloud on her decision, sometimes wavering at great length. This often makes for a very impatient waiter, especially as she asks his opinion of what is good—or bad. She wants to be the last one at the table to order (I dunno what happened to ladies first), and even then she'll take her time as if still undecided. As her brother, this drives me up the wall. Her husband—well, as I said, he can be a saint. Al simply shrugs and says that nine times out of ten he'll glance at the menu and know exactly what she'll eventually order, and he'll be correct.

It might take another ten minutes sitting at the table, however, before we all find out.

There used to be a lot of physical mannerisms too, but these are pretty well a thing of the past. An odd quirk might grow into a habit, such as nodding her head, a twitch in her cheek, a compulsive need to do something with her hands, and for most of her life she's had a nervous cough. But then, don't most of us have similar oddities at times, especially when younger? Perhaps, because I know her so well, I noticed such minor habits more keenly. I suspect part of the reason they are now a thing of the past (except the torture in the restaurants) is that with age she has become more certain of herself.

There is one long-time classic sign of insecurity that she has maintained throughout her adult life, and she's going to pin back my ears for mentioning it. Margaret can be very thrifty— or as Tom Smothers might have put it, she firmly believes in the ancient frugal system. This is likely a trait that developed from a need for both security and stability, sought for by people who have gone through uncertain times. I've seen this frugality in older clients, many of them fairly well off, who have lived through the Great Depression. What would I do if there's suddenly no money? I can't let go of my security. I mustn't spend money unnecessarily.

An understandable attitude, certainly, but Margaret was not always consistent in her parsimony. An emotional plea for help, especially if children are involved, might loosen that grip to some small degree, and yet she never had any children. (An odd statistic. For the past couple of generations on my father's side, none of the women ever bore a child—there were at least five, and all were at one time married. Coincidence?)

In her post-high school days Margaret would horde her paycheques for a couple of years, then quit her job. She would put enough money aside to provide for a safe and secure return, then spend the balance on global travel. This was a cycle that lasted fifteen years or more. Like so many things, however, this can be interpreted in many ways. Perhaps Margaret was simply adventurous and wanted to see the world. Perhaps she just couldn't settle down after the abuse and needed to be forever on the move. Take your pick. It could be either or more, but this globetrotting young woman seemed inconsistent with the petite, nervous girl I knew. Perhaps this was a part of her growing up and sorting things out. And perhaps this entire paragraph is nothing more than a brother underestimating his sister, because Margaret wound up doing a lot of gutsy stuff in the first decades of her adult life.

Regardless, the money would pile up as she worked for two or three years as a secretary, spending little beyond the necessities, with the occasional splurge. Her social life didn't suffer in the meantime, though. Like any single woman she would go out with her girlfriends, and when she felt like it, she was never short of a date. Nor did Margaret have a problem finding a job, being good-looking, easy to get along with (most of the time) and competent. But after a certain period of time she would suddenly quit without any thought to tomorrow, and just go somewhere.

She would always travel by herself, but there was usually someone at the other end. A friend might be expecting her in Sydney, a cousin in England, and there were the new friends she always met along the way. She might end up in Europe or back in England, or simply stay for awhile in a place that was warm. A few times the journeys proved quite adventurous. She once booked a Pacific cruise with a ticket that ended the journey in Australia. She more or less settled there for a while, working mainly as a secretary, though she also did a bit of a walkabout that included such odd jobs as working at a hotel shop on the Gold Coast. She spent a good deal of time in New Zealand on two different trips, and in between found herself working in New Guinea, where she had a boyfriend who was a pilot. She circled the globe that trip, finishing up in England for a while following several years on the trail, before finally coming home.

For most of her life, however, the romance side was a shambles. That brief marriage was to Jacques, a resident of France, in the mid-seventies; and both before and after there were several other failed relationships. Ironically, and in characteristic human fashion, when she was quite young and working in Edmonton, a young lad did fall head over heels for Margaret. He was a really nice young man called Ray, but she merely "liked" him as a good friend. Typical!

When she reached her forties Margaret decided she needed more direction in her life, and this time she channelled her savings toward further education. She earned a BA in English and Psychology at Simon Fraser, and obtained a teaching degree, after which she taught grades one to three in the Vancouver Lower Mainland. She was quite suited to looking after young children, and did well at her job—the same job that led to her marriage to Al. They've been together now for nearly twenty years. My sister retired in 2010 at the age of sixty-three.

CHAPTER TEN

The fallout—or the lack thereof …

Margaret's bombshell about our father's assaults required a major adjustment in my thinking. The first thing it did was take the "me" out of the sexual abuse, for it seemed natural, right away, to let her know she wasn't alone. I think she was relieved to discover this. Perhaps the second realization was that my father was not just as queer as the proverbial three dollar bill, and his oldest son simply a young male within convenient reach of his homosexual tentacles. His deviances were more widespread, and much more heinous than I'd imagined. When the abuse had centred only on me, what was happening had been bad, yes, but once it had slid into the past, it no longer seemed to be that great a problem. It had been a nasty period in my life that was over, something to forget about—just like a protracted period of caning, perhaps—and now it was time to get on with my life, which was going pretty well. But now, no…

***

Marie and I had met when we were respectively fifteen and seventeen. We dated on and off for the best part of a year, then started going steady. When she was seventeen, we got engaged. When she was eighteen, we got married. Three years later we had our first child, and the years in between were pretty darned good. We were just a couple of kids, really, and while there were hardly two cents to rub together, we were in the same boat as all our friends. That makes a big difference. In the meantime we had total freedom to do whatever we wanted, which was great, because it usually didn't cost anything anyway. Drugs were not prevalent in those days, hardly any of us drank more than the occasional beer (we figured sophistication was a bottle of Baby Duck—chilled, of course), none of us longed for lavish entertainment or travel, and our only indulgence was smoking (two bits a pack and we quit a couple of years later). There were few responsibilities, and life was a lark.

A side story on our marriage, one that shows how much times have really changed, and demonstrates how society in those days had its head in the sand about the realities of sex, and young people. About two weeks before our wedding day, Marie and I booked an appointment with my family doctor. We wanted a prescription for birth control pills, which were relatively new at the time. We stumbled into Dr. Miller's office, red-faced with embarrassment, and sat across from his desk. As I began to ramble through the reason for the appointment, because Marie sure didn't want to say why, Miller held up his hand to stop me. "You're here for birth control pills, aren't you?"

We both numbly nodded, turning an even deeper red if that was possible. But his next comment was astounding: "Well, I'm sorry, but I don't prescribe birth control pills. In my religion we don't believe you should be getting married until you can afford to have children."

Sanctimonious prig, and he was being damn well-paid for it too, on my MSI premiums! We left his office even more embarrassed than when we entered, somehow feeling that we were the ones who were being unreasonable, and should be ashamed. Question: *Do you ever have those little daydreams as a more mature adult, when you wish you could go back and have another word with someone?* Dr. Miller would be high on the list. By the way, a week later Marie obtained a prescription from mother's gynecologist, and this time she went by herself.

It was maybe halfway through those first three years of absolutely no responsibility that my sister told her story. And wow, what to do? The abuse struck me as being far more serious than my own, because Margaret was a girl. And I don't think that's being sexist, but pragmatic, even if I didn't know that at the time. Never mind the feeling that this was far, far more iniquitous than what had happened to me, such a notion is well supported by statistics.

With a girl there is a much wider range of negative issues, from the offensive loss of virginity, something that was almost sacred then, to a high risk of the complete dismantling of the victim's life as far as regular relationships with men. This in the long term can mean loss of trust and the further risk of instability within the girl/woman's own, future family. There can be many similar long-term effects for both genders, but the evidence is there. Sexually abused girls will suffer more than the boys, both short- and long-term.

As to the abuse inflicted on Margaret, my immediate, gut reaction was to confront Father. I did that the same afternoon, as soon as I could catch him alone. Why alone? Stupidly enough, both Margaret and I felt we needed to keep this from Mother, along with anyone else, probably because we felt that this "problem" could still be handled—and eliminated. This, as anyone familiar with pedophilia will tell you, was a total waste of time. Such confrontation without the authorities does nothing more than make sex predators more cautious, and therefore more careful. It is nothing more than a warning jerk on the leash, but it's one that doesn't change the nature of the jerk on the other end. Only the police knocking on a sex offender's door can stop him, and in nine times out of ten, even that's only temporary. A pedophile can only be stopped by keeping him off the street or under complete control. Beyond that, nothing can be certain!

Right from the moment that Margaret shared her story, our choice of remaining silent wasn't a conscious decision, it just happened. Neither of us said, "Let's keep it quiet and handle it ourselves by talking to Father and threatening him." It just seemed the correct thing to do. In fact, at that time it was probably the only thing we were capable of doing, so we did it. Looking back, the choice to keep the sordid secret was not made for ourselves, but mainly for the good of everyone, both the family and Mother. "What would she do if things flew apart? How can she possibly manage? And besides, surely we can handle this!"

So, the "big secret," for the time being, remained exactly that, and the silence continued.

Only much wiser minds would have realized that really, it wasn't "our" secret, it was his, and our course of inaction was the worst thing we could have done. But again, we did so with the rationalization practiced by most folks when caught up in this kind of problem. It begins with the delusion that once confronted and even threatened the offender, because he's family, will listen and stop what he's doing. All the other, more mundane reasons have already been mentioned several times over. Mum with two younger kids to raise, how could she carry on; the publicity, all over the newspapers; shame all around, etc. etc. The only reason now added was the most idiotic of all, the notion that we were actually doing something positive, and maybe we *could* prevent him from abusing in the future.

I cornered Father soon after Margaret's admission and we had angry words. By then I was taller than him and probably weighed a few more pounds, but his demeanour never even hinted of physically squaring off—which I half-expected. Instead he oozed contrition, swearing that his "terrible behaviour" was already a thing of the past. He showed remorse too, deep remorse, along with crocodile-like protestations of regret that truly sounded sincere. I questioned him about my younger sister

Angela, who was nearly thirteen. He claimed shock at the very idea, and denied any improper behaviour, even when I told him we were going to ask her if anything had, indeed, happened. I never asked about Steve, because he was only nine years old and such a thing never crossed my mind. As it turned out later, there's a damned good chance that it should have.

About then, I actually threatened him, and told him that if anything were ever to happen to Angela, or to my younger brother, I would kill him (a statement I repeated many years later as a witness in a courtroom).

My father didn't react angrily to the threat at all, which surprised me, because it was a pretty drastic warning (and totally empty). Instead his reaction was just the opposite, and at the end of a rambling litany of promises and explanations, he had the gall to say that perhaps his behaviour was just an odd way of expressing his love for us both. My reply to that included the words, "a crock of shit," and that more or less ended the conversation. I repeated, less angrily, what would happen if he did anything like that again, and warned him that Margaret and I would be keeping track of our younger siblings. The warning did not extend to going to the police or any other authority, however, because I don't think that such an option occurred to Margaret or me. Today that sounds strange, but there you are. There's no point in offering reasons or excuses. That's how it was.

And yes, one other thing. It never occurred to Margaret or I, then or later, that our father would extend his predatory activities beyond the family. Such an act was completely beyond comprehension, because to do such a thing was simply too much to believe. It would have been insane—no matter how you define the word.

***

We kind of pussyfooted when we talked to Angela, in case Father was indeed telling the truth (and we certainly wanted him to be, which didn't help), for our sister would wonder what on earth we were talking about. Nor did we rush in and interrogate her. In fact, we didn't sit down that same day and ask any questions. With tempers high and Mother home, it hadn't seemed like the time and place. Over the following days and weeks, however, Margaret and I talked to Angela, but casually and without being too specific. In fact, they were really no specific questions at all:

How are you and Father getting along?
Is there anything you should tell us?
Is there anything happening that you don't like?
Does he do anything that you don't like?

Nothing raised a warning flag, which in retrospect isn't surprising. That sort of evasive, understated questioning, especially from older siblings, wouldn't have had Margaret or me spilling our guts either. What it would have taken was an older adult conducting a kind but firm, no-nonsense question and answer session that contained a few salient nuggets of explanation. A clever lead-in to the truth wouldn't have hurt, either. I know with either Margaret or me, such a tactic would certainly have worked. There's nothing like convincing someone that you know exactly what's been going on to get them to open up, even if it's just suspicion cloaked as the truth.

Heck, that's basic training for parents teaching their own kids not to lie, isn't it—even if such tactics are blatant hypocrisy? For example, my mother would have had the entire story from both of us years before if she'd only said something like, "Graham, I know your father has been knocking on your door in the middle of the night, and coming into your bedroom. I *know* what's happening when he's in there, too. How long has this been going on?" Presented in this manner, the question slips from asking if anything is going on to demanding how long it's been happening. One doesn't have to be a lawyer or a CIA agent.

With Angela, as it turned out, such a tactic would have been irrelevant. Much later, when Father's behaviour became public,

Angela firmly stated that nothing ever happened between her and Father. As for Steven, Margaret and I spoke with him as he went through his teens, but whatever probing questions we asked were plainly not specific enough to loosen his tongue. Steve, for whatever reason, just clammed up, denying that anything odd was going on between him and Father. He denied that right up to the year of the trial, over two decades later, and then he told everything.

***

Marie and I left soon after the confrontation with Father, and by then everyone, including Margaret, seemed to have found something else to do. As the two of us were putting on our shoes at the back door, I reluctantly explained what had happened to Margaret, and what she'd said about being abused. With my sister's story finally told, there seemed no point in keeping my own quiet. Besides, Marie was no doubt curious about what all the terse whispering and goings-on in the hallway had been about. Even so, I was still oddly reticent in revealing my past. By then, keeping silent about anything to do with Father was pretty much ingrained.

Marie did not at first believe what had happened with Margaret. Having caught part of that quite vicious argument in the front room that had been the catalyst, she thought maybe Margaret was just telling stories. So, figuring I might as well get everything off my chest—Marie was probably going to find out anyway—I told her how he'd picked on me, too. Surprisingly enough, she seemed to take that part of it in her stride, including the quickly censored explanation of what had happened, because to say much more was still uncomfortable. (When we discussed matters later, she said the information was simply too overwhelming to absorb all at once.) Oddly enough, it was a relief to finally speak about it, and now, in one afternoon, I had told two people.

Over the next week or two, Margaret and I figured we had done everything we should or could do, which left no other course than to wait and hope for the best. To reiterate the preposterous, it never occurred to us to go to the police. The possibility was never even raised. Nor was the idea of Father going to jail. It never played a part in our unspoken decision to simply carry on, watch Father, and take him at his word, but keep an eye on the two younger kids.

Putting this to paper today distills all this rationalizing to its essence: an unspoken decision to not make a decision. Yet for the moment, everything did seem to be going along fairly well. Father swore that what happened to us was a thing of the past. That seemed to be confirmed, at least in part, by Angela's response. In the meantime, the rest of the family seemed at least economically viable, which almost certainly was part of the reason for complacency. Father was working and bringing in a regular paycheque for the first time in recent memory, and Margaret herself was doing all right, too. Let neither of us upset the applecart. Let's, instead, just watch out in case it begins to look as if the applecart might be tilting a bit. In hindsight, this was of course a ridiculous hope. You don't wait for an applecart to tilt, because by then it's scattering apples all over the marketplace.

And yet ... the apples miraculously didn't scatter. Life went on, and the only thing that changed was Mother's financial status—which had improved somewhat, though not terrifically. Father continued with his life whilst his two elder children—twenty-one and seventeen years old—effectively, obliviously, protected him. Obvious as it is today, it never even occurred to Margaret and me that this was exactly what we were doing. Like millions of others before us and since, we thought we were doing the best thing we could do for all concerned, including—selfishly—ourselves. A small part of this mindset may have been that we both believed our situation extremely rare, if not unique.

I don't think this was overt "head in the sand" thinking, either. Nobody else had this problem as far as we could see, and in those days there were certainly no Internet sites or agencies out there advertising that they did. Nothing ever showed up in the newspapers or on television about pedophiles or child abuse, leaving us in an unsympathetic, paranoia-tinted void. What Father was doing seemed not to be happening anywhere except to us. And even if it was happening somewhere—as surely it must have been—that didn't tell us what else we should, or could, do. So we did what little we felt we could, and hoped for the best. (Anything sexual that did appear on the news back then would have to be an enormous scandal, though mild by today's standards, such as a well-known hooker being caught in the beds of a gaggle of British peers).

CHAPTER ELEVEN

The roots of a family tree—fungus and all ...

My parents' relationship was different, to say the least. To better understand both of them it might help to know a small part of their backgrounds. And, since much has already been said about Father, a good deal of this chapter focuses on my mother, because in many ways it was her actions, or lack of them, that permitted him to so blatantly carry on the way he did. In some small way her past may shed light on the questions of "how and why?"

Mother was just past fifteen and a half when they met. Father would have just turned twenty-two. In a normal relationship, even in the late thirties, surely a girl not even sixteen should have been near the bottom of such a male's interest list—unless his tastes were a kink off sync? Any such interest should have been further reduced when that girl was as headstrong, self-centred, and poorly schooled as my mother. (That sounds harsh, but it is the truth). Mum's greatest attraction was probably her looks and, perhaps only to Father, her girlish appearance. The old photos from that time show her as looking her age, a young girl just a few years into her teens.

At the time, Mother was also my grandparents' greatest bane, having refused to go to school following the family's move north from London to York, an event that took place in 1937 when she was fourteen. Why my grandparents accepted her stubborn refusal to attend school is another story that will never be known. The question does raise possibilities too many to mention. My mother was effectively raised as an only child and doubtless spoiled, but that alone doesn't explain sanctioned truancy. On the other hand, times were different and her future was likely that expected for working-class women of that period. She would get married, raise a brood of kids, and grow old looking after the house, and except for Father's twisted behaviour, that is exactly the way it happened. As such, maybe her parents weren't concerned with further education, and permitted an unruly child to stay at home because it was the course of least resistance. To my grandparents, seeing Mother married off might even have been a bit of a relief.

Regardless, this is the official story we were raised with and we heard it many times, for Mother told the tale with a peculiar sense of accomplishment, as if proud of her stubbornness. My grandparents, significantly, never mentioned it at all—leading to even more speculation about what really happened. Both grandparents did know the value of a good education, and often told me as much. I think they were even more delighted than I was when they heard I'd become a chartered accountant.

I stated that Mother was raised as an only child, and she effectively was—until a sister arrived when she was sixteen. (We used to kid my grandfather that he'd only had sex twice in his life and got caught both times—you had to know my grandmother to appreciate the comment.) The new sister was named Doreen, though everyone calls her Neen. Mother helped look after her during the run up to her own marriage, which took place a year later when she was seventeen. The two were always very close, to the point of seeming more like mother and daughter.

Doreen is older than I by three years and a couple of months, and in the very early years we lived in the same house because a war was going on. In late 1942, just before I was born, my father was packed off to North Africa with the British army. I was delivered on the last day of December in my grandparents' living room, a home delivery being normal in that era. Mother and I then spent about three years with my grandparents before Father returned and the army demobilized him. As such, Neen and I more or less grew up together those first years, and in many ways were almost brother and sister.

And is this paranoia kicking in again? When I submitted the first draft of this book to my editor, she assumed mother's surprise sister Neen was actually her daughter, not my grandparents'. It stunned me, for such a thought had never crossed my mind, and nor should it, for what seem to be very good reasons.

Neen and I have known each other for more than seventy years, growing up together as kids and later on, as close family as well as friends. As kids, our first years were spent in a close-knit neighbourhood, a small cul-de-sac called Trevor Grove. Everyone knew each other and there was never a hint of anything out of the ordinary—and believe me, the way the neighbours gossiped over the back wall, there would surely have been. Her birth certificate lists as her parents my grandmother and grandfather, and these documents were always predicated by the doctor or, as was usual then, the midwife.

She's my aunt, and I would be quite shocked if she wasn't.

Besides, she's got my grandfather's looks, especially the nose and the eyes and even the set of his jaw.

Yet, though I reject the notion based on these facts, my editor's comments did send my mind spinning in directions never before taken. In fact, in writing a book such as this, the mind frequently wanders paths never trodden before. Perhaps it's best to remain firmly on the old and familiar paths, especially when there is no possibility of following any other trail to its end.

Enough! Back on topic, and to address the comment that my mother was ever "my grandparents' bane." The claim was not made lightly.

My grandfather, an employee of one of several British railway companies operating at the time, was transferred from London to York in 1937—so we were told. Mother would have been barely fourteen. She once told us that she did go to school on arriving at York, attending just long enough to make an appearance. She apparently disliked it even more than her old school in London, and simply refused to go—and that was that! Both grandparents must have capitulated, for Mother remained at home until she was seventeen—then left to become married.

This would have been July of 1941, by which time my father had already been a soldier with the British army for more than a year. The old black and white wedding photos reveal a happy, smiling couple on the steps of one of York's ancient stone churches with the groom in uniform—the itchy kind made of heavy, thick material that is warm as toast in winter, but damned hot in summer. I know because I joined the Canadian Armed Forces Militia during grade twelve, and they were still standard issue even then.

Behind the black and white happiness of the wedding party photograph, however, were two very self-centred people. The first was a pretty young girl—you could hardly call her a mature woman—with a stubborn streak a mile wide, a temper to match, a poorly nourished intellect, and absolutely no outside interests at all. In fairness, the last two traits were not atypical of millions of other young British working class girls of her time. The second was a handsome young man nearing his mid-twenties who, as a supposedly mature adult, had taken up with a fifteen-year-old, and married her two years later.

One might rationalize Mother's teenage interest in such an older man. Her immature mind must have viewed the attention as a real coup. As for Father, one can only guess the motivation behind his attraction. Whatever they may have talked about during their initial courtship we'll never know, but in later life there was certainly no meeting of minds. Father kept busy with his business, his music, some reading, and whatever other pursuit piqued his interest at the time. Mother's interests were the usual for a housewife of that era, focusing completely on the house, the kids, her parents, chatting with the neighbourhood wives (who were all at home), and herself. Even so, in those early days, perhaps my mother and father seemed to have been relatively happy.

A question does raise its ugly head, however. At twenty two years of age, was Father's motivation in pairing with a fifteen-year-old an early indication of the dark side of his sexual interests? Was it even a conscious effort to satisfy interests already in existence?

Whatever it was, their marriage seemed to have attained a state of indifference by the time I was ten years old. By then Mother was openly complaining about her married life, gritty details included, and the children were the handiest audience. It's easy to recall the timing, because first memories of the dissatisfaction are clearly associated with our house on Swale Avenue, a council property that we left when I was still eleven.

Father's indifference did not eliminate the tempestuous aspect of their relationship. As youngsters we saw all sorts of strife. This included such events as my goldfish bowl being upended on Father's head (which resulted in a panicky scramble in search of my floundering fish), dead ashes from the hearth strewn across the living room in anger, tools and utensils thrown against the wall, Father's viciously clawed face inflicted during a snarling scrap, and a roaring struggle in the corner of their bedroom as Mother tried to stick Father with a kitchen knife (I can only recall that single incident where matters reached that level of violence). During this last altercation, I burst through the half-open bedroom door, scared as hell and crying and screaming, which may well have prevented serious injury. It certainly ended the fight.

I never saw my father strike my mother, but she did hit him, and more than once. In fact, once when she was angry with me I managed, just in time, to fend off a swipe with a dinner plate that broke against my elbow. To be fair, that was also the only time that I can recall mother aiming such violence in my direction.

Their scrapping began long before the sexual abuse, and we kids simply took the constant strife as being part of life. When someone is brought up from an early age in a "different" environment, there's a tendency to adjust and take a lot of things in stride. I'll state this repeatedly: kids can be tough little devils, and I think in many ways all four of us were. Who knows, maybe in those early years we really did think such behaviour was ordinary. And again, who knows to what degree it was occurring in the homes that surrounded us? In those post-war council houses full of returning soldiers and young children and young wives, along with little money to spare, the often difficult post-war adjustment, and an education that for most soldiers had ended at sixteen, maybe it was happening with a degree of frequency that might have surprised us.

A good deal of what went on in our home was surely far beyond normal, though. Mother possessed another trait that regularly overwhelmed the minds of the rest of the family, one that has probably become obvious. There were absolutely no secrets. To anyone willing to lend an ear, Mum would reveal all of life's problems and in the most intimate detail, and time and time again. Mum had a terrible habit of constantly repeating her chilling anecdotes, and the audience included her kids. At a very early age we were regularly informed that, among our father's faults, he was not as interested in "that side of things" as he should have been, even though initially we weren't exactly sure what the heck "that side of things" was.

This complaint was just part of a litany of Father's neglect, which seemed to encompass all aspects of the couple's life. In one breath Mother might ramble on to all who would listen, neighbours and friends alike, about the acute shortage of cash, Father's English and Canadian bankruptcies, intimate details of her medical problems, Father's leeching friends, his total amorous indifference, and being forced to leave her parents and come to Canada. In the next breath, it would be the sweet with the sour. She would fondly recall his fantastic tenor voice and what he might have become, but hadn't; how hard he worked at the shop, though he lacked any kind of business sense; and how profitable it had been, yet what money was made got frittered away. The sad part of this litany was that almost everything she said was true. Perhaps saddest of all was that, by the time we reached our teens, my siblings and I and most everyone else she knew had learned to completely tune her out.

But that was only a part of it. Mum was proud of her looks and the attention that was often directed her way. There was never cause to believe she took advantage (until a new lodger eventually moved in), but she revelled in the implied flattery and definitely relished telling about it. Not too surprisingly, considering his inclinations, Father seemed amused by these eye-openers that in retrospect were probably revealed in part to gain his attention. Later in life it dawned on me that he, in turn, might have found a vicarious enjoyment in hearing her stories (hey there, Freud). One incident in particular I recall, promptly related by Mother when I came home from school on a day she had received an unexpected visitor. I would have been about fifteen. It was a story often repeated thereafter, and by Mother, not me. A family friend named Pete had dropped by the house and exposed himself in the kitchen. Details offered all round included the state of his organ, and its generous size. Mother plainly didn't take Pete up on his offer or it wouldn't have been mentioned, but it was clearly the highlight of her day.

Ah yes, Mother told it all.

So no, I suppose we were not a particularly normal family, though on a comparative basis, how far off-centre the pendulum swung is hard to know. Other than the sexual abuse, any other dysfunctions were not particularly noticeable at the time because we were used to them. Kids, as already mentioned, seem able to adapt to a good deal of abnormal behaviour, and if they can learn to at least live with it, they will. I sometimes think that normal went out the window with the last episodes of *Leave it to Beaver*, and *Father Knows Best*. On the other hand, if the behavioural researchers ever pin down a concrete definition of the typical *abnormal* family and take a census, we'd likely find they're in a majority. If so, would that not logically make them normal, and thus define the traditional happy family as abnormal?

Whatever its faults and foibles, our family unit seemed to totter on with little change until one day in the early sixties. A lodger appeared at the door, seeking rooms. Strangely enough, he seemed to fit right in.

Danny, our first lodger after we arrived in Canada, had not accompanied the family on the move to Forest Heights, where the body shop was located. The next lodger, Oscar, was already a friend of our parents when he suddenly found himself homeless. He had either left his wife or been ejected, the facts were never clear, and a divorce was pending. I distinctly recall that Pat, Oscar's wife, had a drinking problem, and that's not just hearsay. I'd seen her in her cups more than once. Pat also had a temper, for I'd seen that too, which was extremely ironic considering the way things eventually turned out between Oscar and my mother. The old proverb of the frying pan and the fire might have been written for him.

Oscar didn't seem to find our family particularly abnormal, or maybe he was just desperate. Regardless, whatever he may have thought, or seen, he kept to himself—for the most part, anyway ... and for the time being.

CHAPTER TWELVE

The time bomb explodes with a silent bang ...

Approximately a decade of complacency followed Margaret's shocking announcement, which took place in 1964. Those years passed in an illusion of relative calm, during which all the nasty stuff seemed to have settled down and gone away. It certainly appeared to Margaret and me that Father had told the truth. As if to prove as much, those ten years began with a family addition that I've so far failed to mention, a younger brother. Mother would have just turned forty-one and Father was forty-seven. Our new brother arrived at the end of August, Mother's birth month.

The arrival was a surprise to everyone, particularly Mother, because she'd had a partial hysterectomy several years before following the removal of a benign abdominal tumour. She thought the operation had made her sterile, but it turned out that only one ovary had been removed. The new arrival was welcomed as the fifth child in the family, though I was no longer at home and Margaret would soon be leaving. His name was Ross.

It might be a good time to summarize the family fortunes during this blissful decade of ignorance, which might be called the not so fabulous sixties. Father's bankruptcy was pretty well wound up by the time the decade was into its second year. He quickly obtained his "B" pressure welding ticket through on the job training while working in the shop of his new employer, a well-known oilfield transportation and hauling operation. The oil patch was healthy even back then. This company, by coincidence, was a client of the accounting firm where I was articling. I was out there with the audit team when my new brother arrived, and I had the unusual experience of receiving cigars—both tobacco and chocolate ones—from my father, as he went through the office handing them out to both employees of the company and our audit team.

As to the job itself, Father seemed to have adjusted to now being an employee, and just how much soon became apparent. Though he had always hated trade unions, he became an ardent supporter. Part of that probably came from working on many of the new oil field projects, the largest of which were union jobs. These were primarily in Fort McMurray, a community that would one day prove to be the site of his undoing. The other reason for his new found enthusiasm may have been that he was British and had a trade. It has always annoyed me when various unions, government in particular, were going on strike, and I'd see a verbose union boss on TV who spoke with a British accent. I mean, just look at what happened over there with their economy....said the ex-Englishman.

Welders made good money in the sixties, and they still do. Nevertheless, funds continued to remain in short supply at home. The lack was a constant source of tension that never went away until my parents finally divorced. It was during this period that the lodger, Oscar, became a permanent fixture around the house and, in more ways than one, a part of the family. My father still shared Mother's bed, though later in life, as other matters bubbled up and finally exploded, both Margaret and Angela claimed that this sharing was quite literal. They would have known. Both were at home until around 1967, and neither was obtuse.

It would have been during the last half of the sixties that Father quit his job at the transportation company and began working full-time at Fort McMurray, at first staying in the camps. It was a boom town then—heck, it still is—and a considerable drive from Edmonton. What drew him there may have been the high pay, or the odd situation at home. What made him remain there proved to be another matter.

Both distance and conditions at Fort McMurray would have been a major life change for almost anyone. Reaching the town first required driving about 130 miles north of Edmonton just to reach the road that led there, which pierced a further 150 miles of mainly Crown land, which is essentially dense, virgin woodland referred to as "bush". This is still largely unchanged except for the paved road. Due to the area's natural topography, it will likely remain that way for a long time, except for the current twinning of that same route, a political issue brought about by the highway's heavy death toll. In the sixties however, constant road construction might cost the traveller a muffler per trip, and once in a while an uprooted rock might even take out a gas tank or an oil pan. It was that bad. Many of the residents were at that time transient with no intention of staying for the long haul, even those who lived in permanent homes rather than the bustling camps. Father seemed to fit right in, and it soon became difficult to know exactly where he lived, Edmonton or Fort McMurray.

This lifestyle continued for maybe the last half of the "decade of calm". During that period, a subtle level of pretense built up regarding Oscar and Mother's relationship, a pretense that seemed to suit all three. There's no doubt that Father turned a blind eye to what was going on with "the lodger," and there was no doubt a variety of reasons for his doing so. Only a psychiatrist with time on his hands might try to explain. Indifference would certainly have been a factor, confirming Mother's earlier assertions. Keeping up appearances might also be included, particularly in maintaining a safe, public status quo as a married man and father. And who knows, this odd, carnal relationship may have titillated Father's peculiar sexual mores. There was a further possibility that was never discussed, one that lurked off in the clouds and remained unexplored. Was a fresh field of sexual gratification being explored in the remote northern town of Fort McMurray, that made the rest of his life simply passé? This last prospect was ignored because, after all, there was no news or even any inference that such a thing was going on.

To be brutally honest, the few people who knew of Father's incest by then —and that had to include Mother and Oscar, as I'll explain—chose to ignore the possibilities. Instead, we all chose to believe that he had reformed. Such a belief was born of self interest and hope. And the hope was maintained and bolstered by choosing not to address his pedophilia (a word that was still foreign) on the basis that, surely, someone in Fort McMurray would have said something if it was still happening. As to his spending so much time in the remote town, why question the silence of something that seemed to be working, and was so convenient?

Incredible, isn't it? Yet the willingness to bury one's head in the sand goes on all the time, even today and by some awfully prominent people, when there is a far greater public awareness of the problem.

Meanwhile, during this period, Marie and I carried on with our lives. Our first child was born in 1966, a boy, and a girl followed in 1969. She was born in Montreal during the two year period when I was transferred by Chemcell Limited to a position as accounting manager for the company's chemical division. (We figure our daughter was conceived somewhere between Winnipeg and North Bay, for she arrived exactly nine months after the move). Our third child, another boy, was born five years later in the town of Westlock, about fifty miles north of Edmonton. We moved there in 1971 seeking a rural lifestyle, which meant my returning to public accounting. It was a move neither of us have regretted.

Margaret did not stay long at home but she did remain in Edmonton, though during this period she lived abroad about half the time, off on one of her global trips. Angela also left home, very early and under terrible circumstances that I'll deal with later. She eventually made her way to the west coast. Steve grew more rebellious, doubtless aggravated by a hostile relationship with Oscar and, by default, with his mother. He dropped out of school some time during grade eleven, and hit the job market.

By 1974 the relationship between my own family and both my parents and Oscar grew more distant, not only in terms of miles but also in its coolness. This distancing had started with our marriage, a natural step. The gap widened considerably with the move to Montreal, which helped us in maintaining a healthy distance on our return. And though this revised relationship (whch rarely included father) may have been a few degrees cooler, for the most part it was reasonably cordial. That's another way of saying that when you're not seeing people very often, you're much less likely to fall into disagreement when you do. As far as Marie and I were concerned, this atmosphere provided a more balanced environment in which to raise our own children when they were young, while still staying in touch with their grandmother. It seemed to work out well except for the very few occasions of prolonged contact.

Considering the larger picture of long-term predator abuse, however, this was utterly selfish. Shutting out the problem with Father and simply hoping it was done with, was optimistic at best. I guess we had all convinced ourselves that the "problem" had gone away, so why attempt to dredge it up? To cite the title of a classic 1959 Ian Carmichael film, I suppose it was a selfish way of saying: *I'm alright, Jack!* (Every Englishman who ever viewed the movie bit his tongue on seeing the title, for he knew the first two words were missing from what was a very old saying: *F**k you, I'm alright Jack!*)

***

Margaret returned to Canada around 1974, following yet another of her "scrimp first and travel later" odysseys. She had clearly been doing a lot of thinking on the return journey, and the history of sexual abuse nagged at her mind. The fact that her mother had stood by as it happened and done nothing was perhaps gnawing at her most of all. As Margaret describes it, the usual stream of complaints and criticism from Mother began all over again the day she came home, a litany that we'd all heard from the time we were young children. It quickly began to grate on Margaret's nerves.

One day, in the middle of a lengthy session, she angrily told Mother, "If you want something to really complain about, I'll give it to you!" She then told Mother what had happened between our father and her as a child. The eruption was long overdue and she deserves credit for finally speaking up. It was something both of us should have done ten years earlier, when confronting Father.

A part of the reason for Margaret's brooding anger was that toward the end of her teens, in an emotional back and forth with Oscar, she pretty much told him of the abuse inflicted upon her. Quite upset, she said, "If you knew what Dad did to me, you wouldn't yell at me like that." That Oscar understood was clear, for later in life he even mentioned to me that, "I told your mum what Margaret had said, and I knew what she meant. But Joan said Margaret was just trying to cause trouble between Rex and her."

Margaret raised this earlier incident with Mother as one of the reasons she felt betrayed, for she correctly assumed Oscar would have mentioned it at the time. (If one ponders on the comment, it was probably delivered in the expectation that it would be passed on.) She demanded of her mother to know why nothing had been done about it at the time. Without question, some sort of horrified reaction would have been expected from a parent on receiving such news; or at the very least there should have been an expression of concern. Most women, surely, would have initiated an immediate grilling of their daughter to at least garner the truth!

Instead, when Margaret did ask the question, Mother merely claimed that Oscar had never uttered a word on the issue. However, when promptly confronted he vehemently claimed that he had, and that she chose not to believe him, adding the words, "I wasn't stupid."

Hmmm, yes…

Caught face to face with the lie, Mother backed down, and in doing so confirmed Oscar's version of events: Yes, he had told her, but she thought Margaret was just making it up to get even with her and Father, though for what reason she couldn't say.

That quick response clearly demonstrates how Mother used to think, though, and where she placed her priorities. It also offers a hint of why there was so much internecine family conflict. And yes, Margaret was betrayed, by both parents.

***

Father's past pedophilia now became acknowledged by everyone in the family except of course Ross, the youngest, who would only have been about ten at the time. However, common knowledge of the crime seemed to do nothing but initiate a Freudian farce. In the end, the only change in the status quo was that Mother's life of hypocrisy finally ended, and Father was out the door. She now claimed belated shock at learning about the sexual abuse, and just as quickly began divorce proceedings. Oscar, of course, although common-law, was standing in the wings.

As far as Mother's initial claim that she didn't believe Oscar, Margaret and I simply treated it with a pinch of salt. Mother must have witnessed everything from midnight wandering and door-knocking, to those sessions in the bathroom in broad daylight—and that was just with me. What she had let slide by with Margaret must have been just as blatant, and should probably have offered even more concern. It's readily apparent that Mother, either consciously or by the deliberate suppression of facts, knew what had been going on. However, if a person were to take a pragmatic view of her circumstances during those earlier times, which she probably did, why would she *choose* to believe Oscar? To do so would only have created huge problems that, in her mind, were probably greater than the ones she had steadfastly refused to face. The greatest irony was that Mother's main concerns were probably similar to the ones that Margaret and I feared as kids, and which had helped keep us silent, too.

There's no point repeating them all, but the critical one would have been the total upset of the family household including all financial support, an issue that for the present had finally settled into a fragile equilibrium—again, ironically. Father was sending money home from Fort McMurray (albeit erratically, according to Mother), yet he seldom actually came home. In the meantime, Oscar was at home every day and doubtless contributing some support for Mother as well as the only child still left at home, my now ten-year-old brother. As the expression goes, she had the best of both worlds, shaky as they may have been in their overlapping orbits.

However, with my sister's words now on the table, Mother had little choice but to acknowledge Father's sexual abuse of his children, which in turn left her little choice but to act upon the information. And besides, as already mentioned, there was Oscar, standing conveniently in the wings. So it was off to the lawyers to begin divorce proceedings. That old TV farce *Soap* could have had roles for all of us!

Divorce is a civil action, often negotiated and settled without recourse to the judgement of a court. Speaking from years of experience as a CA, I'm of the opinion that it's usually best if you can settle out of court on a knowledgeable and reasonable basis. You never want to appear in front of a divorce court judge. Quite often it's a crap shoot, particularly in the days before the reforms of *The Divorce Act, 1985*. In my father's case, however, there was no room to maneouver. He had to agree to a negotiated settlement, or go public and appear in court. Since the last thing he wanted to do was appear in a public civil court, which would have doubtless led to criminal charges, justice was not served. To put it mildly, Father was not in a position to try and make a deal, he simply gave up everything, though in actuality that wasn't very much.

At this point, it's worth looking at the justice system. In settling the divorce agreement only Mother, Father, and their lawyers knew what was openly discussed behind legal counsel's closed doors. Only our parents and their lawyers would have been aware as to what extent father's "problem" played a role in reaching the settlement. Nontheless, each one's lawyer would have certainly known about my sister's allegations, as no doubt they knew about mine, because I'd backed up Margaret's story with my own. Mother, in turn, definitely told us both she had informed her own lawyer why the divorce was taking place. And, being Mother, it was a given that she had also told everyone else within her circle of friends and relatives the full story. So now the whole sexual abuse issue *appeared* to finally be out in the open, and *seemed* about to go public, and Father *apparently* was about to face up to his past.

Yet my parents and the lawyers on both sides kept the lid on it!

It's easy enough to see why the lawyers would have maintained their silence, and more than that, perhaps even rationalized it. To begin with, all client-lawyer information is privileged and private. Beyond that, however, Father's predatory sexual abuse was only 'revealed' in the form of allegations, and as such was hearsay. Nothing had been proven in court. *Ergo*, he wasn't a criminal until proven guilty. In the interim, since everything between lawyers and clients was confidential anyway, there was no necessity to report this to the police, etc. etc. Justice, then, was not served at this time.

Nothing officially saw the light of day. This was despite Mother's compulsive need to tell one and all, which she did, only now it was with a certain satisfaction. More than that, it fully justified the decision to leave father and immediately take up with Oscar, should anyone ask what happened. This attitude resulted in a particularly sad occurrence when she made a point of informing my father's sister, whom she had never liked, and it devastated the poor woman. Marjorie, a timid, innocuous woman who lived most of her life in England as a spinster, was very fond of my father. There was absolutely no need for her to know. The only reason we discovered as much, was Marie and I visited her in York the following year. With tears in her eyes she asked me if it was true. What could one say? Yet there was absolutely no need to pass such information on to Marjorie, but of course Mother felt compelled.

And life moved on. Father's past was now on the table, even if it was in private, and he quickly signed the divorce agreement. Father avoided alimony, but Mother kept the house, which was the only real asset the two possessed after thirty-four years of marriage. That may sound as if it was very little, and it was, but this sort of financial status was not uncommon for the ageing post-war urban generation. Most of the population from that era had never held employment that included a retirement pension (by and large, that was and still is the privilege of politicians, employees of the civil service and larger, well established corporations). In those days the average couple spent most of their lives simply raising kids and paying off the mortgage in an environment of very little inflation. On retirement there would be the old age pension, a mortgage-free house that was usually very basic, some Canada Pension and, if they were lucky, a few dollars saved after the kids left home.

What actually went on behind the scenes at the lawyers' offices? As a guess, when they were signing off on the agreement with their legal counsel, an unstated, undocumented part of the deal probably involved an understanding that Mother would not initiate charges on the pedophilia. Ironically, nobody saw fit to consult those it had directly affected, namely the two known victims. Maybe they figured it was none of our business—and we certainly did nothing to indicate it might be. We just assumed that Dad was finally going to face the consequences ... only he didn't. In retrospect, looking at the cast of characters it's easy to see why.

Despite Margaret's unburdening, the crime itself remained buried; and now, having now been unburdened, Margaret had no inclination to raise the issue again.

Ignoble as it may sound, I had no appetite for waking an angry dog that had been dormant for so long; a dog that, hopefully, just might be dead anyway. (Hmmm..)

Mother probably couldn't or wouldn't do anything because everything had settled out very nicely.

Oscar—well, he hadn't said a word to anyone but Mother so far, so why start now?

Angela was by then off on her own making a living and she'd emphatically stated that there had never been any abuse anyway.

Steve—well, at the time nobody knew, except possibly Oscar and Mother, that he may have been sexually abused, for he still denied everything and was keeping his mouth shut. (He would have been about nineteen at the time.)

The lawyers would no doubt claim client confidentiality if child abuse charges were laid by a third party and enough said about that silly bit of nonsense. Justice isn't embedded in the legal system anyway.

And finally there was Father. He sat through it all blithely and convincingly assuring everyone his sordid activities were, indeed, a thing of the past; that he truly regretted his aberrations; and he had indeed reformed.

Father, until the day he died, was always a very convincing liar. Other than the one time when he was forced to stand up and plead guilty in court or be faced with fighting a lost cause and a greater sentence, he still maintained the lie. (During the divorce negotiations there's a good chance that he might have convinced his own lawyers that his abuse was indeed a thing of the past—if they hadn't bought his sincere insistence that it wasn't true in the first place.)

And so our lives once more settled into the usual status quo of silence, only Father was no longer part of Mother's family. Mother sold the house and purchased a twenty acre parcel of land close to a lake about thirty miles west of Edmonton. Oscar, who had worked for the city of Edmonton as a carpenter, had recently retired and effectively built the new house by himself. I don't know what went on behind the scenes, but title always remained in my mother's name. And yet—you've got to shake your head at this—for quite a while after, Father blithely visited Mother and Oscar at the acreage as if nothing had changed.

Fort McMurray officially became his permanent residence, where he plied his trade and earned a good wage. Money continued to slip through his fingers and did for the rest of his life. Where it went, only the gods knew, and they said nothing. What made me aware of this ongoing problem was his request that I co-sign for a new truck he wanted to buy, for his credit was bad even with the automotive industry. This was a few years after the divorce. I agreed but, not wanting my own credit to slide sideways as a guarantor, I insisted the contract be drawn up in my name, and the payments be drawn on my account, a monthly outlay for which he would reimburse me. That way I'd not be in default, should he fail to make the payments.

He never missed one.

Some things, however small, can change.

***

Over the years following the divorce, Father became fairly well-known around Fort McMurray, primarily because he agreed to put his name to a business that sold investments and prepared personal income tax returns. (Professionally qualified accountants are not permitted to do this due to conflict of interest, i.e. one cannot give objective tax advice when one profits, for example, from commissions made by selling RRSPs.) The business was called G.R. Clews & Associates, which was the first time my father had ever used his initials instead of just his middle name: Rex Clews. This was no coincidence. For many years I had been using the name G.R. Clews, Chartered Accountant, as my practice name, albeit in another town. At the time Father opened the doors on G.R. Clews & Associates, however, my name was associated as being a partner in a well-known firm of Edmonton accountants that had a branch office located in—*Fort McMurray!* (We also had offices in Barrhead, Westlock and Whitecourt.)

This confusion only got me in trouble once, when an Edmonton lawyer complained to the Institute of Chartered Accountants of Alberta that I owed one of his clients thousands and thousands of dollars. This single case of "mistaken identity" was easily dealt with, and only a mild irritant. My main annoyance was actually with my own professional governing body. The woman who phoned me from the Alberta Institute of CAs sounded as cold as a dead mackerel and just about as friendly (I like to imagine that she also looked the part). She spoke in a cool, acidic tone that echoed presumed guilt, before I could even get a word in. But then, accountants tend to be like that—very suspicious. Our clients make us that way.

As to G.R. Clews & Associates, the strange thing about the business was that Father only held a small minority interest. The "Associates" actually controlled the company. To anyone with experience in this sort of thing, giving up your name to be used as a business front and receiving a pittance in return should be a warning. But then, that was Father. He always liked to have his name out there, which seems actually silly considering the more sordid part of his life. If someone is engaged in any sort of sexual misconduct, it probably would be wise to keep the public profile well below the radar. Mind you, look at Clinton, Kennedy, Profumo, and a thousand other politicians.

G.R. Clews & Associates' business operations were probably legitimate for the first while, but the operation finally folded after it became involved in a Ponzi scheme operating out of the same office. At its peak, this scheme was so crazy that the local banking community was actually taking the company's in-house, sixteen percent debenture certificates as security on loans made to purchase the same worthless instruments. Amazingly, no charges were ever laid against anyone, probably because by the early eighties so many businesses were going bankrupt across Canada the system could not have coped. Accountants all across the country were seeing their clients in financial trouble, and the rule seemed to be that if it looked like there was no cash to be recovered, what was the point in spending money to petition a debtor into bankruptcy? If anything was left the banks had it secured anyway, and that was patently true. Official bankruptcy statistics for that disastrous period are phenomenally understated, because most failed businesses simply closed their doors, and not a whimper of their final agony was ever officially recorded.

As such, Father walked away from the whole mess scot-free. Had he not, it would have been a laughable sort of justice to find him doing jail time for running a Ponzi, when he should have been behind bars for pedophilia. On the flip side of the coin, if a person takes into account the sentencing practices of the times (and those of today), he'd have probably spent more time in jail for the Ponzi!

From the published details of the scam, and on meeting the backers, I sincerely believe my father was being used as a patsy, with the principals likely pandering to his ego. And that's not a case of self-delusion, it's fostered by professional experience. He knew virtually nothing about the business itself, choosing instead to relish the importance of having his name on the door and in the papers (*before* the business went sideways, anyway). An individual called Don F. seemed to be in charge of the operation, a fellow who once had the gall to visit me in Westlock and ask my firm to do the year-end accounting work and serve as financial advisers for—that's right—G.R. Clews & Associates. (The answer was a definite no!)

The business lasted from the mid- to late seventies until maybe the mid-eighties, and as far as I know, Father's main contribution was the name on the door. He certainly never had any cash to invest. And I do know for sure that when it did close, he was once again without funds.

One other item of interest requires mention, one that in the long term turned out to be the most important of all. During his years as a Fort McMurray "businessman," Father developed a keen interest in boxing, a sport to which he had previously paid not the slightest attention. This occurred, as far as we knew, toward the end of the seventies, when G.R. Clews & Associates seemed to be doing well. Thinking back on it today, however, perhaps this interest began when he was first working in the north, perhaps as early as the end of the sixties. Taking this one step further, it probably played a factor, perhaps the key factor, in his spending so much time in Fort McMurray in the years leading up to the divorce. In fact, in writing this down, it seems almost a certainty.

Whatever the motive and the timing, somewhere along the line Father must have acquired a good deal of knowledge on the sport, because he became a fairly well-known boxing coach. He was knowledgeable enough in the art (or science) of coaching to develop some pretty good young boxers, who brought quite a few trophies back to Fort McMurray—and continued to do so even after G.R. Clews & Associates had folded. In fact, around 1987, Father was elected to the Fort McMurray Sports Hall of Fame, an honour of which he was inordinately proud.

Almost immediately the bubble burst again, this time with a tremendous splatter. The gods have a merciless sense of humour when it comes to timing.

CHAPTER THIRTEEN

My sister Angela, who triumphed in the end …

When everything finally erupted, and the dust began to settle, it turned out that my sister Angela was the only one of the four children to state that she had not been sexually assaulted by our father. It was, however, probably a close run thing…

Angela is eight years younger than I. She, too, was a good-looking girl, though dark-haired, taking more after her mother. She still is, even in her sixties, though the hair is probably no longer as dark. I can still remember the day she was born. English housewives would have called her a "blue baby." The ambulance came rushing to the house in Swale Avenue, bells ringing—no sirens then—and the oxygen already flowing as they rushed her and Mother off to the hospital. Needless panic, as it turned out. She was fine and the pair soon came home, both as right as rain. There's nothing like a little excitement to start out in life, or for the occasion to stick in a child's memory.

How, later in her life, did Angela fit in with Father's predatory child abuse? Well, she apparently didn't.

The final reckoning for Father came toward the end of the eighties, when he was arrested in Fort McMurray. Twenty-five years before that, when Margaret told me of her own abuse, my sister Angela would have been turning thirteen. This was the age I had once naively considered as being the "dangerous period" due to Father's 'homosexuality", but not for Angela, just for my younger brother.

Angela states categorically that nothing ever happened to her, though she did reveal to Margaret, when asked, that there once may have been a half-hearted attempt that she easily rebuffed. She confirmed as much to me, when writing this book. What actually happened seems to have been a bit of a grey area. The way Angela remembers, it may have been an effort to start something that she quickly stopped by the expediency of getting up, and leaving. She's pretty sure he was masturbating in the darkness, and he may have attempted to show himself at the same time. Whatever it was, Angela says that she ignored it as she stomped off, and nothing else ever happened. It would appear that she was certainly not subject to the abuse that occurred with Margaret, or Steve, or me.

I don't believe Mother, even once she was 'officially' aware, asked Angela if she was sexually abused when Margaret broke her silence. I'm pretty sure she didn't ask Steve either, who would have been about twenty by then. Take that for whatever it means regarding mother's possible awareness. As for not asking Angela, it would have been nigh on impossible to do so by then. Soon after Angela turned fifteen the two rarely saw each other again, because Mother ejected her from the house following a fearful row. Even so, I just can't imagine Mother raising the subject of abuse with her youngest daughter. To do so would have opened too many doors on a relationship that was never a good one. Had Mother even obliquely asked the question, I can well imagine my sister's caustic response. I certainly wouldn't have blamed her.

Later in life, the antagonism that existed between the two resolved itself through the practicality of just not speaking to each other. This situation was not unique within the family. As we became adults, we all settled conflicts with Mother by just getting on with our lives. It was not unusual for at least one of us to be "not speaking" to Mother at any given time, and of course, by default, this meant not speaking to Oscar. To be honest, those interludes helped bring more calm to our own families.

I would guess this state of affairs began when Mother reached her forties and one by one we began leaving home. There were lengthy periods when any one of the five kids might be alienated from her, including our youngest brother, Ross, who is twenty-two years my junior. With Mum, that's just the way it was. Family conflict was always an "all or nothing" situation; or as President Bush might have phrased it, "You're either with me, or you're agin' me." This attitude followed her into later life when, at around sixty, she would change her will to exclude one child or another because they had "offended" her, or did not fall in with her point of view. Upon her death three of her five children plus her sister Doreen had been effectively removed as her beneficiaries (which was almost irrelevant, because Ross secured power of attorney following her final stroke, and virtually cleaned out Mother's not insubstantial bank account).

Mother died in May of 2012 at the age of eighty eight, though no longer completely *mentis compos* following a stroke two years before. She improved somewhat during this period, but not enough to fully recover her faculties, and she lived out her time in a full-care nursing establishment. Oddly enough, as she slowly recovered from the stroke, we noticed that her personality had changed. She became more pleasant and agreeable than any of us can ever remember.

I mention these mother-daughter disagreements to help in understanding the falling-out with Angela, and her almost lifelong rift with Mother. It also helps explain why Angela was closer to Father as an adult, for he was the only one of her two parents who came near to treating her with any sort of sympathy. To use that word again: ironic, isn't it? Nonetheless, her teen years were to prove anything but stable. When family events began to slide sideways for Angela, as they had with Margaret and I with father's abuse, her problems came crashing in from a totally different direction. As far as I was able to see, and certainly as far as Angela is concerned, Mother was the reason she took the route she eventually followed, not Father. Though sadly, he did no more than remain in the wings and do nothing, as he watched it happen.

The constant clashes between mother and daughter began about the time Angela reached puberty. The verbal abuse that flew back and forth, particularly from Mother, was vicious and vindictive. And it *was* verbal abuse, some of it quite harsh, as Margaret will attest, for she was still at home for most of it. It was as if Mother had an intense dislike, perhaps even jealousy and hatred of her own daughter, and continually found fault with everything she did. Of course, it wasn't long before the sentiments became emphatically mutual. The two seemed always at odds, and Angela hesitated far less in spilling what was on her mind than her two older siblings. In this area she and Mother were definitely alike, and the invective flew back and forth like barbed missiles.

Father, if he was around, kept out of it. Even this seemed to aggravate Mother, berating him for not taking "my side." Matters came to a head when fifteen-year-old Angela began seeing a boy to whom Mother took an instant dislike. As many parents of teen daughters are aware—or should be aware, this only served to cement the relationship. As to the relationship and mother, it was akin to a red flag waved before an ill-tempered bull. When Angela refused to give up the lad, she was forced to leave home and became a ward of the welfare authorities. She managed to almost complete high school with very good marks, but with graduation only months away, was forced to leave school because social services cut off her funding. Irony piled upon irony. This would have been well before the divorce, and it seems case officer from welfare had checked on Father's income. He was making too much money, and mother, according to Angela, had in turn informed the welfare department that she was welcome to come home at any time!

At some point soon after, Angela fled to Vancouver. Later in life she freely admitted to using drugs during this time, but beyond that, she revealed nothing much else. It had to have been a pretty tough period in her life.

This mother-daughter antipathy is not, apparently, unusual in instances of what teachers in the school system call "problem girls," a term that doesn't always mean it's the fault of the girl herself. To help explain why this is so, I recall a Dutch war bride called Henny who later became the vice principal of the local high school in Westlock. She used to be a tax client and a good friend. Every year when she brought her "income tax stuff" into the office, we'd quickly leaf through the papers, then sojourn to the local dining lounge for a Tuborg and a steak sandwich lunch while discussing the problems of the world, and life in general. On one such occasion, when our daughter was around eleven or twelve, I bemoaned the fact that she was coming up to those awful teen years, a time that all fathers seem to dread. I won't deny that the problems with Angela came to mind.

Henny grew quite serious, and in her clipped Dutch accent said, "Graham, let me tell you what to watch out for. If there is one trait that runs like a thread through all my girls at school who get in trouble, it's that they do not get along with their mothers."

If Henny's observation fits with anyone reading this, please take her advice. Marie and I certainly took those words to heart. As our daughter went through her teens, if anything untoward cropped up that needed a tough tug on the chain, I played the heavy and Marie kept the doors open. We encountered no problems. In fact, as an adult, Corinna has not only been her mother's daughter, she's also been a really good friend—and mine, too.

As Angela neared the end of her teens, good things finally happened to her, even though they were born of the bad. Before the Vancouver scene, she had been in an accident when riding pillion on a motorcycle. A drunk driver came weaving down a side street in Edmonton, forcing the lad driving the bike to take to the sidewalk. He and Angela were actually up on the grass verge when they were hit. (The drunk promptly slumped down on the curb and downed a few beers, later claiming he'd taken them to calm his nerves. As a result, he could only be charged with dangerous driving and illegal possession of alcohol.) Angela's leg was injured when her heel got mauled in the spokes of the bike's rear wheel. The public trustee sued the driver for damages and held the proceeds, pending the age of majority, which at that time was twenty-one.

When she was around nineteen or twenty, however, the law changed and the age of majority became eighteen. Angela unexpectedly received a settlement from the public trustee. Despite the checkered conditions under which she had lived for the previous four or five years, she completed that last part of grade twelve, then managed to stay the course and achieve a BSc at the University of Alberta, becoming a registered nurse. In other words, she beat the odds. She got her life in order at almost exactly the time that Father's was starting to fall apart.

CHAPTER FOURTEEN

The sound of silence is finally heard…

Once in a while Father would show up in Edmonton or Westlock and our paths would briefly cross, then he'd be on his way. Then, somewhere in 1987 or early 1988, he phoned me. There was the usual social preamble, very brief and oddly tense, soon followed by his reason for calling.

"I, er … I've been arrested."

There was no need to ask why.

My belly gave an odd, empty lurch as a hundred thoughts raced through my mind. The first was, *What the hell happened?* which was ridiculous because the answer was obvious. All the deluded hopes that "no news about Father is good news" promptly vanished. It was replaced by an automatic concern over the consequences of the arrest, including selfish fears about what this would mean to me and my family. The irrational fear of headlines was still on my mind (they never did happen), along with unwanted public embarrassment, especially in a small community such as Westlock (nobody mentioned a thing). Then, as common sense finally kicked in, I felt an odd sense of relief that the dreaded had finally happened—though I'm loath to admit that any such feeling followed on the tail of those initial concerns, not ahead of them.

At the time, the best I could muster was, "I see."

A long silence followed. When it became clear that I wasn't going to say more, mainly because I didn't know what to say, Father got down to the real reason for calling. In retrospect, brash as the question might sound, it was to be expected. "I was wondering if you could lend me some money for a lawyer?"

The second silence was longer than the first, mainly because my brain was mush as it fumbled to figure out what to do. When I finally fathomed a reply, it was probably the best of several possibilities—after all, he was my father. "Sure, as long as you plead guilty." There was no need to mention what he should plead guilty to.

"Hmmm."

Again the silence. While it wasn't precisely clear at the time, this was definitely not the reply he wanted to hear, but he didn't argue the point. I don't remember what exactly was said, perhaps a few more words about nothing, but I didn't ask for any details—and, in retrospect, I guess that was because I didn't want to hear a long tale of woe, littered with lies. His final words before hanging up were that he would get back to me.

He never did.

The next time I saw him was in a courtroom in Fort McMurray. And that was all that happened: *I saw him*. I never did speak to my father again. That was his choice, not mine. Well, sort of, anyway ...

***

The RCMP is responsible for policing Alberta outside the province's major cities, and so Fort McMurray fell under their jurisdiction. The local Fort McMurray constabulary carried out the investigation, but the headquarters in Edmonton, K Division, became quite involved. The awaited phone call came from a detective in Edmonton, politely asking if I would mind dropping into the office on Kingsway and Ninth, to answer a few questions. I said yes, and we arranged a time.

Some time ago a commercial was running on television dealing with child sexual abuse. It bears a very poignant comment from one of the victims—or someone who appears to have been a victim, rather than an actor. The words are simple: "*If someone had only asked.*" Now, so many years later, this message strikes home like a hammer. I did not hesitate in agreeing to drop by. After such a long silence, I viewed the coming interview with profound relief. I would have been about forty-five.

One point cannot be overemphasized: I believe that most children, properly encouraged, will readily answer questions that pertain to their abuse, if put to them by a sympathetic authoritative figure under benign conditions. Most are probably just waiting to be asked just so they can get it off their chest. I'm quite sure that by the time I was, say, sixteen, I would have certainly fit into that category. But while a sympathetic ear is critical, the difficulty obviously lies in determining which kids need to be asked in the first place. I suspect this problem is now compounded by the fear of registering an incorrect complaint regarding the possible sexual abuse of a child. This conundrum is likely abetted by a legal system that might possibly demand damages from anyone who does make an honest mistake. Yet if a suspected abused child is not questioned, the potential damage down line can be far greater. (I do understand that legislation exists to help protect a concerned informant, particularly if it is in the course of their employment.)

It is far from easy, otherwise. A victim of abuse, whether still a child or later in life an adult, has to be tremendously proactive in order to take that first lonely step and report his or her abuse if not prompted. Encouragement is almost a necessity, for it's a major, major decision. This is especially true when the victim has been silent for years, and is now an adult who has fallen into a mindset that finds it far easier to leave matters undisturbed. The current publicity and openness does help, but there's probably nothing better than direct encouragement. To put it another way, it takes a firm prod to get a victim to boot that sleeping dog. After all, the animal has been comatose for years, so what is the point in stirring it to life, particularly if you're afraid it might turn on you and bite? The pedophile relies on this, and Father was a pedophile.

Once the RCMP began questioning, people began to talk. Even my younger brother Steve, who by then had done the whole scene—drugs, booze, motorcycle gang and criminal record—finally showed his hand, telling his story when asked. All it took for all three of us, the third being my sister Margaret, was that pointed but friendly questioning by an authority figure—someone who could be trusted. We probably all found it to be a catharsis.

My interview was one-on-one with a male police officer, and took maybe a couple of hours. He'd clearly done this before, and he was very good at it. The office itself was probably set up for just this type of interview. It was actually more of a small cubicle, very private, with a table arranged so that I sat off to the interviewer's side, rather than across from him. (Even at a civil examination for discovery, a neutral table is usually used rather than a formal desk, to avoid any perceived intimidation by a figure of authority. And, when the situation is one-on-one, it is considered preferable to sit to one side rather than directly across from each other to avoid the sense of confrontation.)

At no time can I recall being really uncomfortable during the questioning, despite the very personal details involved in what had happened. In a way, it was like talking to your doctor. My response was to tell him, in much briefer detail, what has been described earlier in this book. The officer noted my commentary without blinking an eye, though he did home in on the two times that Father sodomized me. He asked if I was thirteen or had I turned fourteen or more at the time. Apparently this was a more serious crime if the victim was thirteen or under. I was unable to answer with any certainty, but it was probably after I had turned fourteen, which was only six months after we arrived in Canada.

After the interview I was asked to sign a statement, and for the time being, that was it. The officer mentioned that in due course there would probably be a trial, though a preliminary hearing would more than likely precede this, and it would be in Fort McMurray. That suited me fine. Even at that late stage, I have to admit that it was a case of the farther away, the better.

Nothing seemed to hit the papers after the arrest, though one of my friends—I had to initiate the topic—said there had been a piece in the magazine *Alberta Report*. I later found the article, a three inch, full-width rectangle at the foot of the page that included a small photograph, and a description of Father as "a polite, mild-mannered Englishman." I had to smile, because nobody had mentioned a word in my home town, though I'm sure the news went around. You have to live in a small community to understand this. By the time Father was arrested, though, I was middle-aged and a tad wiser. It no longer bothered me that other people might know what had happened. By then the main problem, which bothers me even more today, was the impact of not coming forward far, far earlier.

The call to be a witness came in the fall—October or November I think, because there was snow on the ground in Fort McMurray—and just as the officer had predicted, a preliminary hearing came first, to determine if the evidence warranted a trial. Most of the family came up to Fort McMurray for the hearing. Margaret and Steve, who had provided statements on their abuse were there to be witnesses. My mother was there presumably as an interested party, and even Oscar, now her common-law husband, had made the trip. Other witnesses also waited, including one known to us from Edmonton, but we never learned how many more and in what age group, for they were never called.

There was a good deal of apprehension when we three siblings arrived at the courthouse, not because we dreaded the hearing, but having to face Father eye to eye as his accusers. Sounds silly in retrospect, but even at that age we all felt the same way. Yet sometimes matters play out in such a manner that you wonder whether they are happenstance or preordained.

The prosecutor had selected me to be the first witness, and I was shown to a tiny holding room outside the courtroom door and told to wait until called. I'd been inside the room less than five minutes, the door partly open, when Father arrived. He must have been out on bail for he walked into the courthouse lobby in civilian clothes, accompanied by a well-dressed woman I didn't recognize. There were people all around and he stood to one side, just beyond the open doorway to this little holding room. Close as he was, he never looked inside, so never knew I was there. But he stood well within earshot and the resulting conversation was just what I needed to hear.

I can't remember the exact words, but I do remember the tone and the message. Father was still denying everything in a baffled voice that was so very, very sincere. While I cannot recall verbatim what was said, this is pretty darn close: "I don't know why this is happening. I've never, ever touched anyone like that in my life. I don't know why they're doing this to me!"

The woman standing beside him, possibly from his lawyer's office, simply nodded, her face expressionless. They exchanged a few more words before moving away, but those I had already heard were more than enough. The exchange took maybe a minute or two, and if anyone had written such a scene into a movie script they would have been accused of rigging the plot to ramp up the emotion, because for me it was like receiving a breath of fresh air. Any lingering doubts or guilt about testifying, and to be fair, I don't think any remained, promptly disappeared.

There had been an earlier meeting with the Crown prosecutor and a pair of RCMP members who had wanted to discuss strategy. Coincidentally, the young prosecuting lawyer was originally from Westlock, and his father was one of my long-term clients. I'd first met Charlie when he was still a youth. It's a small world. He and the Mounties wanted me to take the stand first for a variety of reasons. I was a relatively successful professional nearing his mid-forties, well-dressed and presentable, and with no apparent emotional axe to grind. They felt I'd be credible and less likely to grow upset than any younger witnesses and, as such, more liable to remain calm when the defence played hardball in trying to discredit the testimony—something Charlie warned me was standard practice in cases such as this.

Nobody gave me any prompts about what to say, from the standpoint of trying to put words in my mouth. There were a few gems of general advice, however: listen to the questions carefully; think on your answers before giving them; don't allow yourself to be rushed or rattled; don't volunteer information just respond to what is asked. And a warning: their strategy will be to get you flustered, so remember that and try not to let it happen.

And with that I entered the courtroom, took the stand, and was sworn in.

Father sat perhaps four or five paces in front of me, just off to the right. Not knowing what else to do, I nodded to him with a very tight smile. He gave the barest acknowledgement, a slight shift in expression that only I and probably the judge saw. His features were already set in a glare (no exaggeration), but his jaw clenched even tighter, drawing his mouth downward in a dangling horseshoe. *Right, then, so that's the way it's going to be!* Father continued to glower for the entire hour or so I stood on the stand.

The odd part about giving testimony is that you very quickly forget where you are and who is there, and simply answer the questions. I had given testimony in court several times before, usually in the capacity of an expert witness on behalf of a client. It's not that difficult, as long as you know what you are talking about. And once the nerves settled and the questions were flowing, I found Father's hearing little different.

The prosecutor went through his agenda, which were pretty straightforward: what happened, when, where, etc. The interesting thing here was that when I spoke of the time that Margaret told me of her abuse, the defence lawyer promptly rose and objected on the grounds that my sister was another witness involving another charge, who would be testifying later. As such, my comments were out of order for several reasons, one being that my testimony would be hearsay. The judge allowed the objection, and the questions continued. Pretty soon, however, my answers once again stumbled straight into my sister's involvement because it fit into the sequence of events leading up to confronting Father, and how I learned of her abuse. Another objection came.

I turned to the judge and said something like, "Sir, it's difficult to keep the two apart. It's all mixed in together with what happened to me, and how I found out about what happened to my sister."

The judge nodded and agreed, this time overruling the objection. I was allowed to relate how Margaret first told me how she had been abused by Father. Soon after, though, I said something that perhaps shouldn't have been said, but it was in response to the judge himself asking a question for clarification: "What did you actually say when you confronted your father?"

My answer was: "I think I told him I'd kill him if it happened again." I unconsciously added the "I think" part because it was, after all, a threat being admitted in open court—besides, can one ever be totally sure, word for word, what's been said in the course of a heated discussion? Hmmm.

The judge, bless him, simply raised his eyebrows and told the prosecutor to continue. Which Charlie did, and it didn't seem long afterward that "the good guy's" questioning ended, and "the bad guy" stepped up to the plate. Looking back, neither set of questions was that bad, and the defence lawyer, I can't remember his name, seemed likeable enough and would probably have been an interesting fellow with whom to share lunch. Nonetheless, he had his job to do.

His first tactic was a memory test. Should the results have been inconclusive they would presumably have served to discredit my recollection of events. Some of the queries were basic, such as the date of our immigration to Canada, the name of the ship, the name of my home room teacher in grade nine when we arrived, and maybe half a dozen others in a similar vein. They proved easy enough to field, and the defence moved on (it may sound immodest, but I have an excellent memory—back then, anyway; today, it takes a little longer, but it's still pretty good).

Father's lawyer next walked me through the actual abuse, and his questions became fairly explicit. It didn't take long to understand one angle he was playing: was there any possibility that I might have actually relished the experience, and perhaps even led my father to do what he did? That part of the questioning was probably the closest I came to being angry, and at one point I did snap back at the lawyer. The tactic made me wonder what Father had told the man. Perhaps he'd suggested that it had never been his fault, that maybe he'd even been encouraged. Such a ploy would not have surprised me, only I couldn't imagine him admitting any such contact to begin with, even to his own lawyer—for surely it would prejudice his defence? I still wonder about that part. Maybe the questions had another purpose.

I apologized for the lapse, tried to relax, and said I realized he was just doing his job. The poor man couldn't prevent the hint of a smile at that, nor could the judge, and perhaps this helped. Father's lawyer seemed to ease off after that. The questioning became more or less general and it was soon over—almost.

The defence lawyer returned to his seat and began gathering his papers. The testimony was evidently finished and I looked around, wondering what to do next. The judge, however, wasn't through. He turned to me in a friendly, almost fatherly manner and asked, "Mr. Clews, what kind of effect do you think all this has had on your life?"

His question was unexpected, and for a moment I was lost for words. What he asked was valid and completely answerable, yet even all these years later I have a problem dealing with such a query, unless I'm quietly going over it in the recesses of my mind. As I've grown older, talking about many sensitive issues is emotionally next to hopeless. As I struggled to think of what to say, my thoughts turned to my own children. What I wanted to tell the judge was that maybe I had not been as close to them as I would have liked, because of always being over-cautious about any form of physical contact being misinterpreted.

I think this reaction was the product of unwarranted paranoia. In raising our three children, I have never had the remotest inclination or notion of following in my father's footsteps. Such a thought would have been repugnant. But I had gone out of my way to avoid even the smallest gesture that the kids, or anyone else for that matter, might take the wrong way. I never really hugged them once they were no longer toddlers, I had no physical contact at all when they were in their teens, and I'd established a fairly rigid set of rules and regulations in their upbringing.

This way of thinking caught up with me once when my inner feelings did break the surface, and I was quite snappy about it, too. Our two boys, who are eight years apart, were on the couch watching television. The eldest was sprawled lengthwise, as teenagers are apt to do, and the youngest, probably about seven or eight at the time, had nestled in close to him. Both had their eyes glued to the TV when I walked into the room. I felt decidedly uncomfortable at their closeness and before I knew it, the words were out: "Don't sprawl up together like that. It's not right."

The youngest just shrugged and sat up, but the oldest (he was about sixteen) rewarded me with a puzzled, very surly scowl, as if I had implied something quite dreadful—which I had. Years later, when the proverbial goo finally hit the fan over Father, it became necessary to tell the kids what had happened with their grandfather, who by then was almost a stranger anyway. In doing so, I apologized and revealed why I had said such a thing, for it had haunted me ever since the ill-chosen words had spilled out. My eldest son clearly hadn't forgotten, either. He nodded thoughtfully, and murmured, "I see."

To answer the judge's question, however, I began by saying that there was nothing that stood out as having a really drastic effect on my life, then moved on to say something about regretting the distance maintained in raising the kids. I suggested that the abuse had perhaps contributed to all three kids being raised in a greater arms-length relationship than I thought was good for both them and me, but I never finished. My face suddenly crumpled up all by itself, and the tears started coming.

The judge quickly banged his gavel even as he began closing the binder that sat in front of him, and promptly announced that court was adjourned. I stood there for a moment, chest heaving, seeing only a blur as everyone began leaving the courtroom. I was actually sobbing, and it wouldn't stop. Not knowing what else to do, I quickly stumbled toward a solitary doorway off to my left and managed to slip through it into what I think was another courtroom. Thankfully, it was empty. I simply stood inside the door trying to collect myself for one hell of a long time. It was the first time in my life that such a thing had happened.

My brother Steve came in somewhere along the line and tried to console me, and everything gradually seemed to settle down. I managed to get my face more or less cleaned up, and shortly after that, we left the courtroom together. My wife was in the crowded lobby, looking for me. Unlike my brother, she was not slated to be a witness, so she had been in the courtroom throughout the proceedings. In fact, I think it was she who sent Steve to look for me. She had tears in her eyes too, which almost started things up again for both of us. We all had a hug, and decided we needed a good, strong cup of coffee before this damned thing started up again.

CHAPTER FIFTEEN

My brother Steve, may he find his nirvana …

My brother Steve was of slight stature, maybe five foot seven, and he was always lean and forever feisty. On the odd occasion, he could be downright pugnacious. I'm not sure if he was afraid of anything, and he certainly wasn't afraid of authority, a mindset maintained throughout his life. Yet even Steve knuckled under to Father's sexual abuse, and in the long run was probably the one most affected by what happened—and not just due to the abuse inflicted by Father. The condition of his later upbringing could have been used as a social worker's case study.

As with all of us, nobody can say what Steve would have been like if he'd never been subject to both the sexual and emotional abuse received at home—but it lasted longer with him than it did with his siblings—and I'm convinced that it was no coincidence that his life played out as being the toughest of us all. The saddest part was that he fell so far short of his potential; but then, so did his father. Steve was blessed—or cursed—with a high intelligence quotient that never really had a chance to be applied, both as a kid and an adult. He died in 2009 when, of all things, he struck a deer one July evening while riding home on his Harley Davidson.

There's a black and white picture taken in the very early sixties that is still somewhere in the photo albums. Steve would have been about seven or eight at the time. The four kids are grouped together along with a Corgi-cross dog we had named Blondie. The three oldest are displaying the usual "say cheese" smiles, but the camera just happened to catch Steve off guard, for he was usually the first to beam into the lens, (and while doing so, just as likely to raise two fingers behind somebody's head). His expression is so forlorn that even if you didn't know him, your heart would go out and wonder why that little boy is so sad. He probably wasn't, it was just the way he was caught on camera. Steve was usually a happy little hellion, but when one looks at that photo, it's as if the shadows of his later life are written on his features as a tragic omen. If life were a bad movie (and sometimes I wonder if it just might be, for it would explain so much), the director would have slid this in as "foreshadowing."

The sworn statement of the abuse Steve suffered is probably on file somewhere in the depths of whatever storage vaults the Mounties use nowadays. By then, Steve had been in trouble with the law and had a record. After the hearing, Mother relayed an off-the-cuff comment made by a member of the force when she had been questioned: *"Reading Steve's statement,"* the officer said, *"he should have a freebie coming."* From this and unguarded comments Steve himself later made, it would seem that his abuse began earlier, lasted longer, and was without question of more depth. Yet right up until that interview with the RCMP, he insisted that he'd never been abused. Even after the hearing he never discussed those years, shrugging them off as being of no consequence.

And that's fair enough if such a course of action works, which I believe it did for Steve to some extent. I think both of us, independently, thought that there was no point in going over things time and again, unless some form of release can be found in doing so. For both of us, there just didn't seem to be any real need. I think we each figured that to do so was no different than picking at old wounds: they simply bleed and leave an even larger scar.

Yet, as I see that last sentence in print, it strikes me that I might be doing exactly that in writing this book: picking at old wounds. But it is not necessarily the memories of the sexual abuse that pick at a person's mind as he gets older. That aspect never seemed to be a huge problem because it could be rationalized and compartmentalized. Steve and I always knew the sexual abuse wasn't our fault, so why should it have bothered us? No, it is the keeping silent that later nags at the conscience. As a person hears more and more about kids being abused, the buried seeds of regret over not having spoken up simply germinate and grow. It was far too late to speak by the time of Father's court case, for that should have been done right away, years ago. Steve and I both knew that, by the time the hearing took place. Still, that doesn't stem the need to do so even now, and I wish we were actually co-writing this.

As to the many other youngsters that Father had abused, like the rest of us, Steve would have known none of this until the hearing. Heck, until Margaret informed Mother thirteen or fourteen years prior to the hearing, he knew nothing about what had happened to his older siblings, and that wasn't his fault, it was ours. And could all three of us really claim to be free of *all* doubt about what Father might be doing during all those years in Fort McMurray? Wishing something is true never makes it so. Steve doubtless believed he was the first and only one being picked on at the time, just as Margaret and I had believed before him. This would have been particularly tough, for there would have also been the isolation of spending most of his time with Oscar and Mother as he slipped into his teens. But Steve simply plodded on like most other abused kids, both before him and after: he kept his mouth shut, and did his best.

The point that haunts all of us, and probably haunted Steve until he died, was that at any time each of us could have stopped it happening to those who followed. It's a sequence of cause and effect. The longer the delay that occurs with any victim reporting their abuse, then the greater the number of kids to whom it will inevitably happen.

So what is it that prevents people from speaking out, even later in life? What is the difference between pedophilia and almost any other crime one might choose that causes victims and guardians, both young and old, to remain silent? Family break up, yes; shame, yes; the worry of consequences, yes; even the undeserved guilt in being an willing participant, yes! These fears, and doubtless many others, help keep the silence. But is that all?

I would suggest there is one other significant reason, one that kicks in when the abuse is finally, finally over. The child is now a tired survivor, a kid finally free of a horrible and very forgettable period of its life. That child now simply wants this traumatic experience to be buried and forgotten. And the child, with a child's cunning, takes the simplest route to do so: say nothing. Keep quiet. For to the child, the expediency of silence very conveniently keeps it buried, if not forgotten. And later in life, as an adult, it is far too easy to keep it that way: that adult simply continues pushing it out of his mind, and there is no external pressure to do otherwise.

Caught inside his own cone of silence, Steve struggled through the rest of his schooling until dropping out. At the time, his family consisted of Mother, an often absent father, and Oscar—who had, to put it mildly, no patience or sympathy for this rebellious youngster. As an adult Steve, who always disliked Oscar intensely and for good reason, once told me that a lippy back-and-forth between them had ended with Oscar actually hauling off and decking him with his fist—a fifteen-year-old kid, half his size. Sister Angela confirmed this recently, she happened to be there. This was just a part of the other forms of child abuse inflicted on my younger brother, all of which he kept to himself as he struggled to grow up.

Steve possessed the natural intelligence to obtain a doctorate in probably any field he chose, yet it would have required a far different upbringing for him to stay the course. He eventually managed to obtain a journeyman's ticket as a welder after leaving school. It was a trade that could be obtained on the job and without a high school certificate, even if the initial pay of an apprentice was lower for that very reason. This option was similar to mine in that his career choice was one of the few that were affordable at a time when no money was available for full-time enrolment in a college or university. Necessity is the mother of much more than invention.

By the time he turned twenty Steve had acquired a lifelong love of motorcycles, and soon found comradeship in the bike gangs that often go with them. He became a striker, then a full member of the Rebels Motorcycle Club, which at the time was Edmonton's equivalent of the Hell's Angels. The two organizations were apparently associated. The choice was quite understandable. Like any other close-knit organization founded on common beliefs, such gangs offer a surrogate family that satisfies a need to belong. The best comparison might be the Artful Dodger and Fagan's den of iniquity in *Oliver Twist*, and I smile as I write that, because Steve could well have played the role of the artful Dodger. He'd have been damned good at it, too—both on the Dickensian streets of London itself, and in the musical production that followed. He might never have had his father's voice, but at heart he was always a bit of a ham.

Like our father, Steve could have done well at most anything he tried, particularly if it caught his interest. Whatever project he chose would then have had his heart and soul. He married early, to a lovely girl—both to look at and to talk to—named Monique. She died tragically in a motorcycle accident, when an inattentive driver simply cut in front of Steve on 109th Street on the south side of Edmonton. (In one of those odd coincidences in life, the accident took place right in front of where the Bump Shop had once been located.) It says something that Monique's parents remained good friends with Steve for the rest of his life, treating him like a son. Monique's widowed mother was at his funeral. Steve is buried alongside her daughter.

For quite a few years the motorcycle gang was the focus of Steve's life, particularly following the death of his wife. It was during this period that he picked up a criminal record. I don't know what it was for, and didn't feel it would be right to ask. It must have been a minor offence, though, because I think he received a suspended sentence. I can't remember him doing any jail time.

He eventually remarried to another very nice woman, Wendy. They had two kids, a boy and a girl, but after maybe ten years of marriage they divorced. Living with Steve, from the outside looking in, was an erratic, unreliable life and it serves nothing to say more, other than one small point that's relevant to this account. Steve loved his family, but never seemed to place them ahead of his other interests, a trait possessed by our father in spades. Yet to what extent can blame be laid on him for this, when raised in the manner he was? And that's without considering the terrible abuse received in his second, fatherless home environment!

Wendy moved to the west coast and eventually remarried, and did a darn a good job of raising their two children. They are a fine-looking couple of youngsters who are making their own way in life, and the boy, Steve (we refer to him as Young Steve), is quite startling to look at. Now in his twenties and a member of the Canadian Armed Forces, in features and build he is darn-near a clone of his dad!

There is no doubt that, in his behaviour, Steve was more affected by Father than the rest of us, but how much can be attributed directly to the sexual abuse? Let me suggest this. The erratic path that Steve followed throughout life is classic for that of a sexually abused child. Compound this with what was a hell of a time growing up in a split, dysfunctional family where he was forever at odds with both his mother and her new partner, and it's a double classic. This hostility was compounded by the fact that his new brother, ten years younger, was raised as the child who could do no wrong. That was none of our younger brother's fault, of course, it was merely fact. As for Steve, well, simply by default he became the kid who could do no right. When that happens, read the psychology books. Such a child will seldom disappoint the naysayers. Heck, naysayers are the ones who relish charting such paths.

Did Steve ever have a chance?

If one were to play the devil's advocate, some of Steve's more erratic traits may merely have been due to acquiring some of Father's personality traits. Yet Father in turn could have quite possibly acquired them himself from a background that was equally nefarious. More than anything, such a setting would have bred that deep need to be thought well of, a characteristic that was shared by all five kids to some degree, except for perhaps Angela. She tended to get on with things without worrying about what others thought. With Steve, though, it was more deeply ingrained than the rest, and accompanied by a lifelong desire to be not only successful, but also to achieve recognition.

This did happen among his peers where he was indeed well thought of. Steve could grow quite emotional when recalling some of the better times—as did many of his old friends when offering spontaneous eulogies at his funeral. In fact, as that memory comes to mind, I recall an old one-liner that I'm sure Steve would have found amusing. If he had known how many people were going to show up for his funeral, he'd have had it before he died.

Alas, the recognition and success never happened, but not because Steve lacked the capability. On the artistic side, he wrote poetry and achieved some local recognition with his readings, especially among the elderly. He also published an illustrated children's Christmas book. As for his trade, he was extremely talented, to the point where he built up a fabricating business on the west coast that for a time did quite well. Surprisingly, for most of the time the business was operating he employed Father, who would then have been around eighty. However, just like Father, Steve lacked the hard-nosed, disciplined personality required of self-employed individuals who achieve financial success.

For instance—and this sounds just like our dad—he ran the business from the hip. Let's not bother too much with details such as budgets, planning, cash flow, and sales, sales, sales—let's just make it happen. Alas (and I'm sorry if this sounds like Ebenezer Scrooge), you don't spend any of the cash unwisely, and in particular you don't give it away, not until you've got it safely in the bank and the debts are paid. Like Father, Steve could never say no. Perhaps that's even why he took his Father into his home during the final years when dementia set in.

As this chapter closes on Steve, an incident comes to mind that's a great example of the often "devil may care" manner with which he lived most of his adult life. Perhaps it also demonstrates the impatient zeal he had to just get on with life, and damn the details. Many years ago he purchased a new Harley Davidson, probably on a weekend, a time when it was impossible get it licensed or insured. He took the machine out on the highway (God knows how fast he was going) and hit a rough patch that forced the wheel sideways into an abutment. As Steve told it, the bike went one way and he went the other, each skidding a few hundred yards along the pavement before slowing to a halt. He then climbed to his feet, shook himself off, walked back to inspect the wreckage, then carried on.

Maybe that last sentence could be applied to so many other bad things that happened in his life. He climbed to his feet, shook himself off, turned back to see what could be made of the wreckage, then carried on. That's just one of a dozen stories that could be brought to mind in a half-hour of not too much hard thinking. The Harley story was pure Steve. On the one hand, there was an incredible amount of luck when it came to basic survival; on the other hand, there was a huge pile of self-inflicted bad luck when dealing with the basics. But Steve, being Steve, simply shrugged it off and carried on. Heck, he'd grown accustomed to doing exactly that since he'd been a kid.

When Steve died he'd been with his third wife, Suzanne, for quite a few years and it seemed to have been working well for both of them. Steve would have been in his forties when he met Suzanne, who was a fair amount younger. There were no children. They lived in Mission, BC for quite a while, and our father moved in with them as a boarder somewhere around the time he turned eighty. Steve and Suzanne later moved to Alberta and Father came with them, and they looked after him until his early stages of dementia. Father died about a year and half before Steve.

What would Steve have been like had he never been sexually abused? What would he have been like had he been raised in a far less erratic family? The only answer that can be given with any assurance is that he'd have been a damn sight better off.

Chapter Sixteen

A sentence is more than mere words, but not much more …

The point of a preliminary hearing is to determine if enough evidence exists to go to trial, so I suppose it's a necessary part of the process. Such a hearing can be useful. From what I saw, the format was in many ways a mini-trial prior to the real trial which would likely last much longer and cost far more. If matters can be settled at this stage it saves a lot of public funds in conducting a formal trial, even if the process may sound a bit redundant. In marginal cases, a hearing would clearly prevent wasting the taxpayers' money on a two week trial if a judge decided the prosecution had no case to begin with. On top of that, the accused might quite likely be suing for costs and other damages if such charges then proved to be frivolous.

In a situation such as my father's, however, it was in some ways the opposite. The evidence was overwhelming, and resulted in a quick plea bargain that was effectively an unconditional surrender. The process did save a good deal of money and a lot of unnecessary stress for a slew of witnesses when compared to going through with a formal trial. And it did serve justice—more or less.

Regardless of practicality and economics, however, it is apparently the right of the accused to request a hearing before the actual trial. This is possibly what happened with Father, and it was probably a good tactic by his defence. It would be no surprise to discover that he had vigorously protested his innocence even to his own lawyer, despite so many witnesses standing by ready to provide evidence that testified otherwise. To his lawyer the outcome must have been predictable, as it should also have been to Father, despite protests of innocence that were actually no more than the final wisps of a forlorn yet ever present smokescreen. Had the case gone to full trial, it would have certainly dragged on to the same inexorable conclusion, and likely leaving a very unsympathetic judge to pronounce sentence. The hearing probably gave Father's lawyer an opportunity to look at the cards now on the table and say, "Let's make a deal." I would also guess it allowed that same frustrated defence lawyer to face down his client and say, "Look, Rex, I told you so!" Either way, the hearing probably resulted in a reduced sentence because Father caved in early, and pleaded guilty.

Once the judge adjourned his court the Mounties and the prosecutor, Charlie, quickly got down to business. Both sides acknowledged that sufficient evidence existed to go to trial, without calling on the other witnesses elsewhere in the building. We never knew who the other witnesses were beyond the family. There was at least one from Edmonton and possibly more, but the others, who knows how many, were apparently from Fort McMurray. An obvious guess would be some boys from the boxing club, most probably young adults by then, and possibly some of his old neighbours. As to their numbers and ages, one can only speculate.

The prosecution arranged a meeting in a small room just off the courthouse lobby. Charlie seemed to be the man in charge, but there were two plain-clothed Mounties present who seemed to have input. Father and his lawyer were not there, and neither were any non-family witnesses. My brother and sister were there, and I was quite surprised to discover that Mother had been invited. Why, I don't know, for she was never considered a witness or a victim. Perhaps she was an aggrieved party. Perhaps she was there with an "impact statement" that might be considered in settling whatever sentencing deal was in the offing. Either notion, really, could be considered a bit of a chuckle when considering the past. Whatever grievances Mother had, it was obvious that the sexual abuse had been her children's problem. It had never been hers, not unless it was convenient to claim so.

Father's lawyer had called for the plea bargaining, as mentioned, and the prosecution and the Mounties were quite willing to respond as long as we were so inclined. They pointed out that to accept a plea bargain would save a lot of emotional pressure on the other witnesses. There was also the reality that to run a trial would take a lot of time, cost a lot of money, and in the end might make some difference to the sentencing, but probably not one of significance. These latter two points were not spoken of directly, but more or less implied.

There was a also a minor, mitigating matter that Charlie placed on the table along with the guilty plea offer, and it caused more than one sardonic comment. The defence lawyer had asked Charlie to pass along the information that Father now found himself impotent as a result of a car accident a few years prior. Father would have been about seventy at the time of the trial. I believe the accident occurred when he missed a red light, and his car was T-boned. The family knew about the accident, but not the alleged damage to his libido. The implication was that, since he was impotent, he was also presumably sexually harmless, and this should mitigate the recommended sentence. The topic was never brought up again, though I did wonder how much investigation had gone into the claim.

My siblings and I said we would go along with whatever the Mounties and Charlie felt was reasonable. After all, this was their area of expertise. Mother seemed ready to throw the book at him though, and the Mounties appeared to sympathize then pretty much left her alone. By then I figured they had the family history pretty-well pegged.

A discussion followed as to what would be an acceptable sentence, which came as a further surprise, for we had no idea. I think each of us thought, *Why are you asking me?* This was not exactly our area of expertise. After all, we had no idea whether a sentence for this kind of crime was one year, or fifteen. Had we been aware of the process, we might have arrived more prepared. Even so, how do you sit down and discuss how many years you want to put your father in jail? Because when all's said and done, that's what it boiled down to, and he was our father. At best, they should perhaps have let us know what they thought it should be ahead of time, and we could then give our reaction. Even at that, it would have probably begged a further question: "What's the going rate of jail time for this kind of thing?"

This was over twenty-five years ago and perhaps even Charlie and the Mounties were unsure about certain aspects of the sentencing. Nonetheless, this was where Mother's input was asked for, and her response implied that anything short of hanging was acceptable. Charlie had a somewhat lesser sentence in mind though, somewhere around two years, and that was finally decided as the punishment. Personally, I thought it wasn't very much. Not for what he'd done to me, but for what he'd done to so many others. Nonetheless, it was apparently the standard of the time. And even if it wasn't, what else can you say? "Naw, no way! I think we should put old Dad in the slammer for at least another ten years, just to teach him a lesson!"

Later on, one realizes that there are other reasons for this get-together on the sentencing. First and foremost it was probably about permitting the victims to participate in the judiciary process, particularly the part that involved deciding what to do with the person who had victimized them. There would also have been the ancillary benefit of possibly forestalling any subsequent complaints that the prosecution was being high-handed in cutting a deal all by themselves. It has to be that way, and I agree with that. Heck, when we left that room it was with the impression that if we weren't satisfied with the deal, we could actually initiate a full trial. If that was true, which in retrospect I doubt, then I still feel it would have been a waste of money. More importantly, it would have caused yet another round of emotional trauma for any younger witnesses who may have been waiting. They had already had enough of that.

In order to fulfill the agreed terms of the plea bargain and in order to avoid a formal trial, the accused has to stand up in court and plead guilty. To ensure that there is no misunderstanding as to the offence(s), he or she must also agree, under oath, to the basic details of each crime for which a guilty plea is entered. That would have been the part that Father likely found most galling. It would mean publicly denouncing every lie he'd told from the very start of the process, including the convincing prevarications in the lobby of the courtroom, and probably a host of others uttered elsewhere. When he was done, the judge passed the expected sentence: two years. Or it may have been two years less a day, so he could serve his time at the provincial jail in Drumheller. I understand this is where most sex offenders are sent, if not all of them, perhaps to protect them from a less than sympathetic prison population incarcerated in Alberta's other jails.

As with most pedophiles, throughout the entire confession my father apparently never displayed a shred of remorse. In fact, I'm sure he pleaded guilty under self-imposed duress, and it wouldn't surprise me if he was still telling his lawyer he was really innocent. And that is not written to be mean, nor is it casting a handful of vengeful stones, for I don't think I ever felt mean or vengeful about my father. It was just that I knew him so well, and having read various reports on convicted pedophiles, I'd learned that the insistence of innocence is not only endemic, it also borders on the psychopathic. Nonetheless, I firmly believe that Father was not fooling himself. He knew he was lying. He just never could bring himself to admit to his crime because, well, something like that could ruin a man's image.

And by the way, following the hearing and the sentencing, the newspapers reported hardly anything, other than those in Fort McMurray, perhaps—but I didn't go looking to find out.

CHAPTER SEVENTEEN

Why do people do the things they do?

There is much about my father that I would like to know, but never will. He died in January of 2009, and just about everyone in his generation is also gone—and if they aren't, they soon will be. Give us another couple of decades, and I suppose the same morbid meanderings will apply to those of my generation. Add a decade or two to that, and ... well, it makes you wonder what it's all about, doesn't it?

Truly, from time to time, one has to wonder: What is the point of it all? Of the really well-known people that history remembers, the names that slip most easily off the tongue are those who have spread devastation and war, heroes or otherwise. (Try: *Constant Battles, Why We Fight*, Steven A. LeBlanc). If a person created a list of the most important and memorable characters throughout history, it seems the infamous would far outrank those who have brought benefit to our world. In the meantime, the rest of us, those hundred billion human beings born in the last fifty thousand years, just fade away. And in the end, what does it really matter, even for those who were once famous?

The Sound of Silence

Everyone, even the heroes of history, makes the same journey, with the same aches and pains and tragedies, and with the good times wedged in between. And while it's all about different actors playing the same old roles, one must ask if matters are gradually improving? I'm not being maudlin, I'm just trying to make a point, and it's a positive one. Today, in the Western world, society is slowly changing for the better, and on nearly every front. Let's hope that other elements in the world don't screw it up.

Among the many improvements we find is that with child abuse, especially sexual abuse, the crime receives far more of the overdue attention it has always deserved. Oh, there are holes in the fabric. Those predators "afflicted" with such tastes travel to other parts of the world, such as Thailand, to satisfy their perversions. They do this in an environment that has so far proven safer for them than the country in which they reside, and they have often been successful. Yet even in those countries with a history of serving as safe havens for the sex offender, law enforcement is changing, albeit at the pace of a snail—a tiny creature notorious for the slimy trail it leaves. One day these nations, too, may get their act together ... if they can stay ahead of the corruption.

Some people may disagree with the use of the word "afflicted" in the previous paragraph to describe the criminal urges that drive sexual predators. Such disagreement is understandable, because "afflicted" might seem to offer the pedophile an excuse for his behaviour. To wit, if a person is "afflicted," the term echoes too much of "disease" and suggests that the 'victimizer' is not fully responsible for his actions—which incongruously is correct, but only in part. Yes, pedophilia is a mental disorder that is accompanied by a horrendous craving which is extremely difficult to control, but to gratify it crosses a distinct line that makes it a crime.

That's tough, very tough, for the future of any individual who, through no fault of his own, finds himself a pedophile. In some ways his inclinations, as far as their being part of a life choice, are no more an option than people who find themselves to be dedicated heterosexuals or homosexuals. However, there is no other way to deal with an active pedophile than to clearly make what he does a crime, and punish accordingly. For it is a crime, and a particularly heinous one, too. There are few others, if any, that inflict greater short- and long-term emotional damage on their victims.

What must be realized is the vast gap between a pedophile and those who are not. The pedophile, usually through no fault of his own, has acquired a perversion that is extremely harmful to children and to society in general. This does not make him insane. Take a typical, random definition of "afflicted" as found from various dictionaries on the Net: *ill, sick, affected by an impairment of a normal physical and/or mental function.* That's why the word "afflicted" is used with a pedophile—because it fits. To revert to the vernacular, this means that the pedophile clearly has an impairment of mental function, but he ain't nuts. If not for his pedophilia, he would more than likely be the same as any other member of our society, which is a huge part of the reason he goes undetected, as my father did for so long. But, to reiterate, once the pedophile gives in to his damaging urges (or mental disorder, if you prefer), it becomes a crime.

One might loosely but effectively compare this to the urges that haunt an alcoholic. Being an alcoholic is no more of a crime than *happening to be afflicted* with pedophilia. But if, in giving in to his craving for drink, the alcoholic turns violent and assaults or kills someone, the result is a crime, pure and simple, and it was likely caused by being an alcoholic. Similarly, the pedophile can gratify his cravings all he likes through fantasy, but if he gratifies them through child pornography or the assault of a child, then that's a crime. The pedophile is and must be held responsible for the control of his urges, *or he simply cannot live free within society.* While that might sound like colossal overkill to some people, having lived with and intimately known a serial pedophile, I believe it to be true. Further reading only serves to confirm this.

It should be noted that I did not say "must be permanently incarcerated," but rather "cannot live free in society." These words translate as this: if the pedophile cannot control his urges, then he himself should be controlled. (If the violent alcoholic cannot stop drinking *and beating people,* for example, then he should also be controlled.) It really all boils down to rights, doesn't it? Yes, a pedophile has the same rights as any other human being, and he darn-well should. I believe, however, that a pedophile's right to remain at large are trumped by the right of children to be safe in an adult society. This has to happen, even if the poor bugger had no choice in being afflicted with his pedophilia in the first place—but difficult as it might prove to be, he does have control over his urges.

When the rights of one person are exercised to the extreme prejudice of another's, then there has to be a social balance. There is a name for that: justice. It seems as if this is sometimes overlooked in some of our court rulings, particularly at The Supreme Court Level. (Personally, I have long felt that at least five of the nine judges should be non-lawyers, with complete access to legal assistance for the finer points of law; to do otherwise leaves all of society's key decisions in the hands of a very narrow cross section of society—lawyers.)

While the comment about "cannot live free in society" echoes of smugness and overreaction, there are two important facts that cannot be overlooked. The first: *there are huge numbers of pedophiles living in our society, more so than nearly everyone realizes, i.e., people whose sexual preferences are for children. Yet the vast majority of these people never cross the line and actually inflict their preferences on children. They keep their urges under control.* (Loose comparison: most alcoholics don't go out and beat people or drive when they are drunk.) Most pedophiles either push their urges aside, or keep them within the realm of their minds—without the need for pictorial representation, which is a further criminal abuse of children. The second: *an active pedophile, short of physical castration, will virtually never reform.* Like Father, they will just continue on and on.

The word "afflicted," which is appropriate, helps me better understand my father while not having a shred of sympathy for his actions. There are many people out there with often devastating "afflictions" that involve strong urges to commit excess with their mind and/or their body, hurting both themselves and others. The most common is obesity, a condition that is rapidly increasing in incidence in our society. Its negative affects are primarily inflicted on the health of the obese themselves. There is also the alcoholism cited above, a "disease" that will severely damage both the alcoholic and the lives of the people around him or her. Neither is a crime, of course, but both share at least two similarities to pedophilia:

both require extraordinary amounts of individual willpower to control the urges that drive the problem;

both, even obesity, can have a devastating effect on the people who surround both the alcoholics and the obese, particularly their children.

The pedophile, ironically, suffers no harm to himself in allowing his "affliction" to rule his life, while his actions almost always have devastating effects upon his child victims, and just as tragic, upon the victim's loved ones.

With all three "cravings," a significant number of the afflicted just shrug and give in to their urges. But obesity and alcoholism are combinations of physical and mental distress, which result in both an emotional and physical addiction driving the afflicted person's preferences. i.e. both the food and the alcohol physically drive the craving, along with the mind. Pedophilia seems to be driven by a mental condition only, and there seems to be no hard evidence to the contrary. It is probably an addiction though, one that is perhaps the ultimate in selfish cravings in that it always hurts others when gratified. That is why it must be resisted. My father did not.

During the latter part of his life he sank into himself as he grew smaller, and in his final few years developed dementia (maybe even earlier—does pedophilia qualify?) All I learned about his final years I garnered from my brother Steve. I never spoke to Father for the last two decades of his life. This was something he wanted, not me, though it didn't really bother me ... I think.

Nonetheless, I would have dearly liked to ask a myriad of questions, though it's doubtful that many would have been answered: what was the cause; when did it start; what was *his* upbringing; was *he* sexually abused, and if so, by whom; and, regardless of whether or not he was abused, what was it inside him that made him start and then continue?

It's a funny thing, but even as I list just a few of those questions, especially the last one, I can almost see him in my mind as he answers. He is sitting across from me in an armchair and he's maybe about the age I am now. His face grows thoughtful as he ponders the answer. Finally he shrugs, raises his eyebrows as if surprised, and says something like, "No reason really, son. It just happened."

Could anything have been done to stop it? Short of putting him permanently away or under twenty-four hour surveillance, I believe the answer is a definite no.

How did the wrongs he perpetrated sit on his conscience—or better still, did he even have a conscience? Again, I think the answer is a resounding no. He simply gratified his urges at a cost, a very high cost, to others.

And worst of all, at least for me, what could or should I have done that I did not? That is the single question that I can answer, for what should have been done is obvious. It has dragged on my conscience like a plow for the last few decades of my life: I should have spoken up, loud and clear, to anyone who might have listened.

CHAPTER EIGHTEEN

If justice be served, how large, then, be the portion?

A friend of mine spent more than a decade in the RCMP. We used to talk back and forth occasionally about the justice system. One particularly sarcastic comment he used to make showed how much one thing annoyed and frustrated him while he was in the force: "If you ever murder someone, Graham, you might as well bump off anyone else you want to get rid of at the same time. After the first one, they're all free."

In Canada, jail sentences are served concurrently (On December 2, 2011, new federal legislation permitted discretionary consecutive sentences, but only for first degree murder). Take the example of a criminal who receives eight years for armed robbery, three for aggravated assault upon his robbery victims, and another ten for manslaughter because his getaway car "accidentally" killed a teenager while fleeing the scene of the crime. All sentences would be served at the same time. In this case, the offender would at most serve ten years, and likely a third less for good behaviour—an expression that is surely an oxymoron. In the US, sentences are often sequential, so in the instance of a serial killer, he might be sentenced to jail for 150 years. In other words, if he kills two or three times, he isn't ever coming out. On the other hand, if he's in Texas he'll actually be executed, but they only do it once.

In the instance of a pedophile, it's obvious that in Canada the system works the same way as it does for the described bank robber—to a degree. All things being equal (e.g., the level of violence), minor differences might be found in a particular judge's discretion. Even at that, while the multi-victim pedophile would probably receive a longer sentence than an offender who has, say, two charges against him, the difference will not be anywhere close to proportional. Picking figures at random, the person charged with two victimizations might get two years less a day (which puts him in a provincial prison); the person charged with two dozen offences might get five years.

So how much time should a pedophile spend in jail for his crimes? In the instance of Father, what may have *effectively* happened was that he was sent to jail for sexually abusing me. For all the other offences, and God knows how many others there were because I don't know if there were any other specifically named guilty pleas he had to confess to, no added punishment seemed to be given. In other words, he walked out of jail after serving less than fourteen months. Yet had he pleaded guilty to even a hundred charges, it would have made little difference to the sentence, because all hundred would have been served on a concurrent basis.

The public is not as tolerant as the law, which is understandable, for we're talking about people's children. These are children, some of them very young, and particularly vulnerable, who could be our own. Quite frankly, I feel the law is too easy on sexual offenders as far as restraining their freedom of movement, because of the often devastating, long-term effects of the crime. Throughout this narrative, I've probably given the impression that the animosity I felt toward my father was not particularly great, and it wasn't. But that was because the sexual abuse was happening to me, it was something that took place and as time passed I understood the cause, and he was my father. Yet here's the peculiar, but perfectly understandable, twist. Had his offences been inflicted upon my children or grandchildren, it would have made a hell of a difference. Furthermore, and this doesn't make sense at all, I think that difference could possibly have boiled right over if the perpetrator had been a stranger. Not logical, but this is the way it is with a crime of this nature.

And in this instance, the accused was the man who, for better or for worse, was responsible for bringing me into this world to begin with and, regardless of the job he did of it, he helped raise me.

As for the general public's opinion on sentencing, depending on the person one asks, the range may run from life in jail and even hanging to no actual jail time at all, i.e., get thee to a mental institution for lengthy treatment. There would be no consistency. This is why we have qualified, impartial people (most of the time) presiding over the courts, rather than turning such matters over to what could effectively be a sympathetic tribal council or an angry mob. Yet when it comes to sentencing a pedophile, when my father was jailed there was a huge anomaly in sentencing that still, to some degree, exists today.

This anomaly is not restricted to just the length of the sentence. Another contradiction can be found in the traditional sentences handed out in rape cases that involve an adult female as the victim.

Rape is certainly a heinous crime too, and I don't believe for a moment that the sentences being handed down are too light. However, I feel that the pedophile commits a far worse crime, and for two very basic reasons. The crime of pedophilia is rape to begin with, as surely as it is when a rogue male rapes an adult woman. But there is the additional crime of breach of trust in simply being an adult, a trust that is compounded if a parent is the victimizer. Furthermore, there is also the near certainty of creating far greater, long-term emotional damage to the child victim.

Such long-term damage is brutally brought home in the *Little Warrior Society* commercials that offer the stark message that of every four women who take to the streets, three were subjected to child sexual abuse. That certainly doesn't happen with adult rape victims. Yet even today, sentences handed out for first- and even second-time instances of pedophilia are frequently lower than those given to first-time non-violent rape offenders of adult women. I mean, go figure. We're talking about children here.

Father was seventy when he was sentenced. By the time matters were finalized he may have been seventy-one. With almost seven months off a two year term for good behaviour, that's darn little punishment for the swath of damage he caused to other peoples' lives, including those of his children. And if the word "punishment" is deemed to be offensive, then try deterrent. And if that doesn't work, which it will not for those who believe only in rehabilitation for criminals, perhaps "detained for the safety of the public" might be preferable. Since pedophilia is a diagnosable mental disorder, this probably is a better description, but it doesn't change the bottom line. If the pedophile is an active predator, then he needs to be confined somewhere, or somehow controlled, for the safety of small children.

Yet what do you do with a convicted pedophile, considering that one of the key philosophies of the Canadian justice system is rehabilitation? To reiterate: *there is virtually no chance of rehabilitating the active pedophile as long as he's pumping testosterone.* (I found this comment in various forms many times when researching this book). With this in mind, what other choices are there for people who, to put it simply, cannot/will not control urges which they acquired through no fault of their own?

This is particularly grievous in that studies on pedophiles who do not control their inclinations consistently mention there is a complete lack of remorse for the crime. Along with this, the pedophile often comments that he believes he is doing the child no harm and may actually be assisting the victim in the initial introduction to sex. This latter comment struck home, describing my father to a T, all but the word "believe". All I can say, based on my limited experience, is that it's hogwash. They know otherwise! Many psychiatrists may dispute that, but I would still insist, and quite stubbornly, that if that's what they beleive then they are overwhelming wrong, and I'll explain why.

While my father never claimed his actions did no harm, it was also never a point of discussion between us. The one claim he did make about the abuse being a way of showing his love was just a wretched excuse of the moment when being confronted. He never again fielded such a tactic, because he knew it was transparently false. He certainly didn't believe it himself, that was obvious in his expression and the wheedling tone of his voice, but he did figure I might buy the excuse and thus mitigate his culpability. This was obvious in the way he backed off the moment I tossed the comment back in his face. Nonetheless, it does demonstrate how the mind of just about any criminal works, and more specifically the mind of the pedophile: *If I lie convincingly enough, perhaps I'll be believed; and if not, maybe I'll instill doubt; and if that doesn't work, then at least I will create a facade of innocence and hide behind it—for there is no way that I'm able to have people think I did this knowingly, because it's something to be bloody-well ashamed of.*

Father told the lies, barefaced and convincingly, right up to the courtroom door, but he never believed them himself. I'm convinced of that, and if any delusion was involved it was in the fact that maybe, just maybe the lie would be believed. There's a quote of very doubtful origin (variously attributed to Goebbels, Lenin, or Hitler, but more likely a condensed paraphrasing of what all three had heard elsewhere): *Tell a lie often enough, and it will be believed.*

This was Father's instinctive form of defence though it's doubtful he ever considered the ploy to be a formal strategy. He just lied to cover his butt and to place himself in a better light. He didn't care what he said, as long as it might serve his purpose. All of us who knew him never for one moment thought that he believed his lies. We knew him too well. My father was an accomplished liar, and had honed the ability to sound as sincere as a saint in the telling.

Sure, he was basically amoral. But that does not mean he was unaware of the consequences to his victims. It simply means that it didn't bother him. A pedophile with even basic intelligence does not truly believe he's helping introduce some poor kid to sex. What he does believe is that when caught, if he manufactures the self-serving excuse of 'helping' the abused children, it well may mitigate his guilt in the eyes of others. Perhaps equally important, those who are disgusted just might be persuaded in some small way to view him as being a deluded victim as well. And therein is found the greatest paradox and the double tragedy of pedophilia. If one is indeed cursed with this mental disorder, then this latter comment contains a grain of truth. The pedophile is a victim. But being such a victim does not excuse gratifying the criminal urges that go with it.

A pedophile probably never wants to be what he is and this seems to be the consensus of a multitude of psychologists and psychiatrists who have studied the subject. There doesn't seem to be much of a choice in the matter, however, any more than the choice previously mentioned as to being either homosexual or heterosexual. The latter do not rape children, however, while a significant percentage of pedophiles do. When the pedophile pretends that a sick form of loving, guiding pedagogy is his justification, it only adds to the crime.

Father was not oblivious to the damage he was doing. He was simply selfish enough to cast any attempt at self-control aside and indulge his deviance, while still trying to convince all who would listen to think better of him. The trouble is, he was my dad. I had known him since I was a toddler. He was afflicted with pedophilia. Other than that, in many ways, he wasn't all bad.

CHAPTER NINETEEN

There's the bad, sure, but then there was the good …

As mentioned in the previous chapter, I feel that my father knew what he was and that he was certainly bright enough to know the damage he caused. I don't believe he rationalized any of this to himself, he simply chose to ignore the facts and the consequences as they applied to both others and to himself. That's probably a good enough summary of someone who's amoral. Nonetheless, he was still my father.

Similarly, there was my mother. Mum was not the most stable person in the world. She often presented a terrible image and example when raising her kids, and she knew and thus tacitly condoned what was going on with Father. She did nothing about that. Yet she was still my mother.

And in telling what happened over the years, the picture I painted of them may seem dark—in fact it's been black—but that's because this book has focused on the child abuse that took place, and the circumstances surrounding it. In terms of days, weeks, and years, this dark side took up only a fraction of the time I spent growing up. Most of those years were pretty darn good. In fact, they were truly good. Most of the time, especially before we emigrated, my parents looked after their family probably as well as, and sometimes better, than other parents of their generation and circumstance.

My early life held many highlights. Before leaving England my parents financed a three year stint in the Boy Scouts that included annual camping trips in the Yorkshire Dales. Before that it was the Cubs. Down by Clifton, we kids fished and swam in the River Ouse. And when we had free time it was truly our own. We could play all day, evenings too, and just made sure we were home for the meals! The only tainted memories during that period were the growing parental rows and those three years at the grammar school. And to be honest, even the grammar school was, for the most part, a good place to be. First the eagerly awaited fitting of a school uniform, then the raft of new friends to be found soon after. There were the sports fields where we played cricket and soccer, and took off on cross country runs. There were annual swim meets, perhaps the only time I ever came in top of the class at anything. Looking back on three years of failure, the main problem was that I found no fun in the "less important stuff", such as paying attention in class and doing homework.

No, life was good for the main part, and as for those five years in Canada before hitting the full time job market, they were most definitely some of the best days of my life. I still get together with some of my high school friends. There's a breakfast meeting on the south side of Edmonton every Tuesday morning with some of the guys, and a small group reunion about every two or three years, with maybe a dozen or more couples attending. If there is a single conclusion with which we unanimously agree when we get together, it is this: you can plow through five thousand years of history and find no better time and no better place to grow up than in Western Canada in the late 1950s!

And as to my parents in particular, there are good memories there, too. My father was the man who regularly took the family to the beach at Scarborough when we were kids, and helped teach us how to swim in the cold water of the North Sea. He held the seat of my first two wheel bike when I was learning how to pedal the crazy thing as it wobbled over the concrete paving of Swale Avenue. He took me to see Laurel and Hardy "live" at the old Empire, when they did a final tour of all the theatres in which they had played. He was the man who snuck a wooden carpenter's bench into my bedroom on Christmas Eve, silently enough that it was a surprise the next morning. He was the one who walked the couple of blocks to work so I could solo the car that day I received my driver's licence—at sixteen. He took me up in that old biplane over London, scaring the dickens out of Mother right after the war ended, and prior to that, he spent six years in the British army helping fight the darn thing. And finally, whether by accident or design, he was responsible for my becoming a Canadian.

Father just never had the proper balance in his mind, and the consequences were drastic. Not for him because, to paraphrase a line from *Gone With the Wind*, Father blithely wandered through life and "frankly, didn't give a damn." His actions proved devastating to his family, and to how many others, nobody will ever know. I doubt if even Father knew. And as the word "devastating" hits my screen, I realize that the hurt to others may have been far worse than it was to his family. The abuse inflicted on me, for instance, was perhaps less than devastating for a couple of reasons. He *was* my father and I knew him and I knew he wasn't all bad. And very early on, perhaps around the time Margaret unloaded, I came to realize that, putting it in plain language, his mind was screwed up.

And as to Mother, she may have been the one who suckered me into peeling those spuds, but she looked after us well when we were young, and saw that we were well fed, decently clothed, and had proper manners. The early days were particularly good, for she seemed to be less self-centred then, and more caring. But then, she was younger and I was younger too, and perhaps both of us chose to recall those years as being better times. Nonetheless, I'm convinced they were.

I remember the many long walks we had along the Knavesmire in York when my sisters were younger, looking for horse chestnuts or romping in the grass. This was the same place, in teeming rain, where she took us to Chipperfield's Circus when it came to town. We kids could almost always cajole her into a pint slab of ice cream when Capaldi's van drove around with its bells chiming. And it was she who would wheedle for us when Dad was digging in his heels. She was the one who, with her parents, raised me during the first three years of my life while Dad was "away at the war". And, toward the end of that war, she was the one who tearfully stood by my bed as my grandfather applied hot mustard poultices to my chest before stocks of penicillin were readily available, and fretted that I might die. And she was the one, for better or for worse, who put up with the darker sides of Father—just as he, in turn, had to put up with hers.

Like Father, she just never had the proper balance in living her life or within her mind. The consequences proved damaging. Not so much to Mother herself as to others, for she was a survivor who was in many ways as oblivious to the feelings of others as was Father. Perhaps in this one instance only, they were a match

When I look at the greater picture, by being the first born, I was very lucky. My parents gave me a pretty good life as I was growing up. Margaret fared not too badly either for she closely followed, but then came those terrible years of her abuse by Father that Mother ignored. Though seeing the words "Margaret didn't fare too badly either" on paper reminds me of that tired old one-liner: *Other than that, Mrs. Lincoln, how was the play?*

However, I made that comment to serve only as a comparison for Angela and Steve as the youngest. They were the two left holding the short end of the stick, Steve in particular. In addition to the sexual abuse, he was raised by a split family that offered little comfort and piles of neglect. Such treatment will destroy a kid's self-esteem, and misshape his outlook on life. Perhaps worst of all, Steve in particular missed all of those enjoyable, relatively normal years before coming to Canada because he wasn't even a year old when we arrived. I enjoyed thirteen of them, Margaret eight, and even Angela got a taste, though was likely too young to remember much of it.

If my father had not been a pedophile, *if* he'd had a bit more business savvy, and *if* he'd had far less ego; and *if* Mother hadn't been so self-centred, and *if* she hadn't been so short tempered and erratic..... Well, I guess life might have been close to perfect.

And as if any other family is perfect, huh?

Oh, well. To quote a long-dead Celtic woman named Elena, "Ifs are only wishes!"

CHAPTER TWENTY

That's all very good, but how do you feel about the "whether"?

This manuscript has forced a good deal of introspection that I had not anticipated before setting pen to paper ("fingers to keyboard" is a better description). The results have not been anything to be proud of, to say the least. This self-denigration is neither imagined nor is it self-pity. It is directed toward the lack of character I displayed in not facing up to what should have been done: reporting Father to the authorities immediately on becoming an adult. Now, more than ever, the omission becomes so obvious. The irony of this (there's that word again) might be found in the fact that my character as a youngster left me with no sense of guilt over the sexual abuse itself, as so many kids seem to experience. Even so, at thirteen, in my mind, keeping all that quiet was totally excusable.

That same brash, overconfident, self-centred attitude, however, almost certainly set me on the path I took as a very young adult of twenty-one when Margaret told her secret, namely the path of silence. Perhaps even at that age, however, ignorance, immaturity and the times may have offered some excuse. Nonetheless, long before Father's deviance became semi-public with the divorce, there was a presumed maturity that should have said: *It's time for your father to pay the piper, just in case he isn't what he says he now is.*

It took middle age and Father's arrest before I finally spoke up, and even then it was only upon being asked to do so by the RCMP. Or, to sum up by paraphrasing another tired cliché: *once the horse was finally back in the barn, I helped close the door.* This reaps nothing but guilt and shame later in life—and yet all over North America enormous numbers of victims, probably most, seem to follow the same path, and many more—God only knows how many more—will forever remain silent. To reiterate, this is what the pedophile relies upon. In fact, it's the only way he can exist. And it's why so many of them can number their victims, quite literally, in the hundreds.

One can trot out the excuses already given, and they are many. And why not, for there have been years in which to rationalize them: family protection; believing the younger siblings' denial of their own abuse; sincere promises from Father that it was a thing of the past, promises that were (conveniently) believed. There were divorce lawyers and other adults much older than I who did nothing and should have done something; and finally, there was the willing delusion that nothing *seemed* to be going on anymore, anyway. There is yet another excuse so far not emphasized: the reluctance to initiate a criminal charge against your own father, or: *How can you send the old man to jail?*

But this doesn't cut it. Looking back, I can see that all those reasons were rationales of convenience, probably in a manner similar to that of Father rationalizing his reasons and excuses for doing what he did. This comparison becomes paradoxical, in that the pedophile once again orchestrates his own perimeter of defence based on the predictability of his victims. Maturity, not simply age, should have brought a re-examination of the consequences of Father's acts. A proactive approach should have been:

Graham, turn your dad in, for everyone's benefit. And if the predator isn't your dad, the same voice should still speak up. In fact, when it does, that just might make doing so just a tad easier if he isn't your dad, but it's still going to be damned hard.

I understand it took a complaint from a resident of Fort McMurray to finally stop Father. I think that even this event occurred sometime after the abuse had actually taken place, so for some time there would have been silence there, as well. Such late reporting might also have meant that Father's claim of impotence following the car accident could actually have been true—which would be yet another irony, in that when finally arrested, he was no longer able to claim any more victims. And while that's a big maybe, it's also irrelevant. Justice still needed to be served, and for many reasons. But in order to make sure that happened, it took someone else to break the silence.

Some form of guilt will likely remain with all of us to some degree, and if it doesn't, then it probably should. There is nothing anyone can do to change that. In my case, and I would guess in most instances, this is a major, unexpected effect of sexual abuse. In the long term, it may quite possibly create a greater burden for some victims than the abuse itself.

As to any other long-term consequences that perhaps did affect me, they might take the form of an occasional wistful moment, pondering what might have been. Thoughts such as, *Wouldn't it have been nice to have had a warm, fuzzy "Father Knows Best" kind of family that offered moral support, the nurturing of whatever gifts with which we were blessed, and parents that tried to set an example that would prove worthy of emulation.* Alas, even Robert Young, the star of *Father Knows Best*, had his problems. He suffered from depression and alcoholism. And Billy Gray, his TV son, later in life claimed the program was nonsense anyway, because, considering the reality of the human condition, it was far more fantasy than truth. Not only that, he believed the themes often disparaged women, and were boring in their content.

Hmmm. So a few bumps needed smoothing out it seems, but that shouldn't stop a person from trying.

Perhaps the greatest loss to my own family was that our children enjoyed the warmth and affection of only one set of grandparents, my wife's mother and father. Sadly, even as kids, our oldest boy and our daughter wanted nothing to do with my mother, who by then was living with Oscar. They each made this decision independently, and for good reason. Once the two of them were past the baby-doting stage, they received little attention from that sector, but loads of criticism. This was particularly true of our oldest boy, and his sister saw it happen.

On the positive side, by then my father was becoming a virtual stranger, and as it turned out this avoided some very real problems that we'd convinced ourselves no longer existed. Oddly enough, when I was a child, a similar relationship existed with my paternal grandparents. Father's parents were perhaps ten years older than my mother's. They didn't mind a visit from their grandson, but they always seemed to remain distant and indifferent. Hmmm...

Mind you, Mother had nothing but bad words for them as far back as I could remember. Once again, in retrospect, Mother probably viewed them as competition for Father's attention. Who knows, perhaps both sides had cause for complaint, because:

> *Every story has three sides,*
> *That form an endless riddle.*
> *One is yours and one is mine,*
> *While truth lies/dies in the middle.*

A couple of comments to close this chapter. There is a one further bit of wishful thinking that sometimes crops up. Wouldn't it have been nice to have enjoyed a warm, romantic, even loving introduction to sex, instead of that surly, sullen Saturday molestation by a furtive father? This and the subsequent abuse left an early, narrowly defined view of sex. If there was a small positive side to Father's continuing intrusions however, it was that it likely did nothing but reinforce my own sexual preferences, which are most definitely heterosexual. Even so, my first notions of what sex would eventually be like with a girl "when I grew up" was along the lines of a pleasurable physical act (coitus), and that's as far as my thinking went. It seemed as if it had little to do with love and romance. I wish the whole learning process could have been different, and normal!

On the other hand, looking at today's young people and their casual acceptance of coitus at a very early stage of almost any relationship, often the first date, maybe my highly imaginative "sex for the sake of it" dreaming were simply ahead of its time. (That was written tongue in cheek, but gosh, when dating a young girl in those days, *we* used to *kiss* each other good night. And I'm convinced it's still better that way, in the long run).

And a final regret. The tragedy of parenting is so often this: by the time we achieve whatever wisdom we might ever muster to best raise our children, they are already grown. The grammar school environment and the sexual abuse I experienced must surely, in unfathomed ways, have had a direct and detrimental effect on how I raised my children. I'm certain of that, even though all three have turned out to be really good kids, and are doing well. I have in fact talked with them about the notion of being too strict, for example, especially with the older one, who suffered the more rigid rules. (Sadly, the first child receives all the child-rearing theory, while the rest receive the all-important benefit of practical experience). Regardless, they all claimed there was nothing wrong with the way they were raised. In turn, one wonders if they just say that to keep the old man happy …

One way or the other, I'd give anything to go back and be less strict and controlling, show them how to be kinder and less rigid than I was, and try to close a distance that I deliberately kept for fear of misinterpretation. A few more hugs, for instance, and maybe a bit more time spent with them doing, well, maybe even doing nothing but just hanging out. There were small but very specific incidents when lessons might have been taught that

I missed, such as encouraging generosity, or simply being less of a prig. But then, I suspect most parents would grab any opportunity to go back and correct at least one or two small failings that will forever haunt them.

I don't think my father would have been one of them.

CHAPTER TWENTY-ONE

A few things worth noting along the way …

Tough Little Devils

Parenting is one of the most skill-requisite occupations in the world, yet the only qualification required is the ability to have sex.

Children are resilient, but resiliency, like everything else, has limits. Long before that limit is even broached, children need help, and the best place to get it is from their family. Yet within a child's family exists one of nature's greatest conundrums. The greater the need for help, such as when sexual, physical and/or emotional abuse is present, the less likely a child's family is fit to provide the help that is so desperately needed. To the child this often means that his or her only choice is 'to go it alone'.

The most precious gift parents can give their children is a caring, stable family home. It is difficult enough to protect our children from the dangers that lurk outside the home. It is far more difficult to protect them from the dangers that lurk within. Flawed as it might be, the family unit is a child's haven in a storm, and if it's lost, he or she is likely to seek out a substitute, such as Steve teaming up with a motorcycle gang. Before that happens, however, a youngster will desperately try to keep the family together, even if the parents are no longer interested in doing so.

Most children, even in dysfunctional families, seem able to develop a form of rationale, or validation perhaps, in which they are able to cope under often incredibly difficult conditions. They will cling to what's left of their family unit as if it were a lifeboat, even if there is a gaping hole in the bottom. And though everyone within sight might perceive that the lifeboat is sinking, the child is probably looking frantically about, desperately trying to find a way to plug that hole.

Kids are tough little devils, much tougher than adults give credit, and often much tougher than the adults who have their care. Couple this with a powerful need to keep their family unit together, and they can also be damned devious. When I was at most ten years old, three years before any sexual abuse, Mother left Father after yet another terrible argument. The reasons were the usual: lack of money (probably true), placing himself first above family (true), a general indifference to my mother (totally true), and who knows what else. Off she went with my two sisters—Steve was not yet born—to live with her mum and dad at their home a couple of miles away, on the far side of a public grazing land called Hobbe Moor. She had never done such a thing before that I could remember, and I felt as if the end of the world was coming.

I dug my heels in and refused to go with her. I would have loved to, because her parents, my Nan and Pop, were the two favourite adults in my world. But I stayed with Father instead. I did it for a firm, solid reason. I knew that if I remained with him, Mother would come back. She would have to, because I knew instinctively that she would never leave me behind.

Oh, what callous little devils kids can be! At the end of the school day I would go to my grandparents' home and eat dinner, then sit at the kitchen table afterward and do my homework. Later, when it came time to ride my bike back across the moor and stay the night with Father, I would pointedly kiss everyone good night before I left—except my mother.

It didn't take long. She was back within the week. You don't have to be an adult to be a real turd, nor do you have to be a grown-up to commit grievous errors of judgement.

There's a reason for telling this story. Kids want to keep their families together, and will go to great lengths to do it. They are even willing to sacrifice themselves in order to do so, though they don't realize it at the time. They do this by keeping their mouths closed and their troubles to themselves, thus perpetuating that cloak of silence on which the pedophile relies. They do it because they feel the need to do it, even though they may be scared as hell. And you can't blame them for what they do. I mean, after all, how do you fault abused youngsters for keeping their mouths shuts when a major part of the motive is to keep their (dysfunctional) families together? Hell, we're talking about someone who is just a kid!

You can't fault them, so you might in turn wonder how they manage to do it, and carry on. The answer is simple. It's because kids are, for the most part, tough little devils. That doesn't mean that in being tough they're not vulnerable; nor does it mean they don't hurt, defiant though they may be. They're just being kids.

Gender and the Abuser

Throughout this small book perhaps the word "irony" has been overused, yet time and again, as I wrote the word, it seemed the only appropriate word available. A further irony has not been mentioned, however, and it's a huge one, and I may get roasted for this. The gender of a pedophile makes a difference in so much as it applies to young male victims.

Perhaps the best reason for this seeming anomaly can be found in the fertile minds of young males approaching, or newly arrived, at puberty, and in how they relate to a potential female abuser. The facts here starkly demonstrate the difference in the perception of this crime, and it's held by many of the people concerned. There is particularly a difference in the minds of young males in general, whether involved or not. There is also a difference in the minds of the mothers of the young males who do become victims, just as there is even a difference in the mind set of the fathers of those same abused young males. And to some extent, there is also a difference in the attitude of society in general.

Even psychologists and psychiatrists do not seem able to agree on this point when discussing the immediate damage and the long-term effects of this aspect of pedophilia. And in raising this issue, please take the comments as nothing more than a pragmatic look at the views held by most young male victims of such abuse, and sometimes those held even by their fathers. The comments are not to be confused in any way as condoning the crime. Even so, even to raise the subject might seem to be skating on thin ice.

The loathing and disgust at being sexually abused by one's father, or by any other male pedophile, are reactions that only someone who has gone through the experience can fully understand, be they boy or girl. For me it was a skin-crawling invasion of body and mind that kills all positive emotions on contact. The first time this happened was in the summer before I enrolled in grade nine. This would prove to be the same grade when, quite frankly, my imagination later began running wild with youthful fantasies which, for example, might well have included being seduced by my female art teacher. I don't remember whether or not she did figure in those imaginative journeys, but if not feel free to substitute the girls' grade ten phys. ed. teacher.

My art teacher was probably well under thirty and extremely attractive, an opinion shared by every young lad at the school.

And yet, had those dreams become an unlikely reality, they would have quite correctly been considered as sexual abuse—pedophilia—by everyone except me. On second thought, you could probably add all my male buddies at school, had I chosen to tell. Considering the close band of brothers that we were—see Chapter Two—I can pretty much vouch for that. Are you beginning to grasp the double standard?

From the pubescent male's point of view, I suspect there was little difference between a sexual fantasy about the cute girl at the next desk, and the one about the attractive young woman teaching the same class. It's all just about having sex, something not yet experienced at that age except in the mind. At the same time, the faintest hint of sexual contact with an adult male would have been totally abhorrent to the same pubescent, heterosexual male, and never mind its skin-crawling physical reality. So in the mind of many a young lad, one form of sexual abuse is deemed horrible, and the other could be quite literally a dream come true. Simple logic would draw the conclusion that the effects left by these two different forms of abuse, both short term and long term, must surely be less if perpetrated by a female offender rather than a male. Not necessarily nonexistent, but less, and perhaps far less.

What is the difference between male and female initiated sexual abuse, then, if there is one at all? Criminally, there is supposed to be none. Perceptively, it seems that a lot depends both on the victim and his family.

In running down a wide range of facts regarding pedophilia, if a single consistency is to be found, it's that figures and expert opinions on almost any topic are all over the map. The various percentages given regarding the number of female pedophiles versus males seemed to vary from 4% to 15%, with the odd one as low as 2%. Comments on "unreported abuse" statistics seem to agree that far more female pedophiles remained unreported than males. If one draws on the example of my art teacher, such comments make sense.

Such a statement about "unreported" abuse, however, must by its very nature be unsupportable. How do you get any figure for any unreported crime, other than by assembling whatever data you have and then taking an "educated guess"? Applying logic to garnered facts is the usual method of arriving at such claims, and in this instance the logic seems to be twofold. First, many sexual abuse victims remain silent anyway, but there must be a supposition that male victims of female pedophiles are more likely to do so because of their "special relationship", and in many instances a predisposition to accept such advances. Second, the crime is generally not considered to be as severe as the sexual abuse inflicted by adult males upon either boys or girls, and that seems to be a fact. As such, once it's discovered by parents and guardians, reporting the abuse is far more likely not going to happen. Maybe the abuse by females is greater than the statistics show.

Going the other way, however, sexual abuse by a female is far more likely to be talked about by the male victims, for the degree of attached shame and guilt, if it exists at all, would be far less than if the abuser had been male. This would be particularly true around school and on the rumour mill, and therefore it would be more likely to surface and be brought to the attention of the authorities. Combine this with the statistics on known male versus female pedophiles (at the most, ten to one), and I wonder. The gap in unreported sexual abuse by females may not be as large as estimated.

Even so, part of the reasoning followed above does lead to a further significant difference in male versus female pedophilia. It's not the crime, it's the punishment. I think that one of the two reasons posited above for not reporting sexual abuse by adult females is that both the victims and their families often do not consider the crime to be as serious as abuse inflicted by adult males. Some people may not agree with this, but I do believe it to be true. This feeling definitely spills over into our justice system. The sentences handed out to female offenders are both consistently and considerably less than those handed out to males. See the Appendix, *A Few Facts*.

A further difference. The female pedophile will nearly always select male children as her target. When a young girl is sexually abused, the crime is almost always committed by a male, but he is often as likely to abuse boys as well. As a result, the male predator will inflict by far the most damage on society, both through the enormously greater number of victims and, quite probably, in the related trauma that results. Personally I don't think there is any "probably" in qualifying the trauma, but I use the word for a reason. When sexual abuse of pubescent boys by adult females is discussed, there seems to be widespread opinion regarding the long-term damage done by the predator. Most opinions seem to agree that while there may appear to be little damage to the young male victim in the short term (it's even acknowledged that a certain amount of youthful gratification might take place) in the long term there will be damage, though here opinions often seem to be vague as to exactly what, and to what degree.

Not too many experts seem to disagree with some sort of long-term effect, though I would emphasize several comments made by researchers to the effect that a lot depends on the individual himself. But then, that would be true of all types of abuse. And if all of this sounds rather inconclusive, it does show that there are so many aspects to sexual abuse of the young that one must stick to the basic tenet. Child sexual abuse is a savage misuse of trust by an adult that, when exercised, is heinous both in the act itself and the damage done to the victim. This is *why* it is a crime.

The Maternal Cover-up

My path has crossed that of two other pedophiles over the years, though technically they were incestuous fathers picking on their daughter(s). Apparently, in such cases the crime laid before the court is probably incest, rather than sexual abuse or sexual assault. In one instance, the mother "refused" to believe her daughter, instead preferring to believe her husband. It was only later in life that the father was brought to justice, and even then it was because a daughter-in-law spoke to the police expressing concern for her child, the offender's granddaughter.

It is no coincidence that when the mother does choose the route of denial, it is often done with her own best interests in mind, consciously or otherwise. Here can be found one of the great incongruities in reporting sexual abuse. The mother will do this for many of the same reasons that a child will clam up when he or she is being assaulted: security, financial stability, public shame, guilt.

The father involved in this instance, by the way, protested his innocence right up to the courtroom door, and even to me when our paths crossed one day at a funeral lunch. Not only were his words exactly the same as my father's, they were delivered with the same pitiful thespian sincerity. His daughter, who I'd know from being a teen, supported her sister in law by affirming that she had also been abused, and the mixed-up scars of that abuse probably carried over into her marriage, which eventually failed.

As for the second incidence, that was truly odd in two ways. The first was that the father went halfway to admitting what happened, implying that the alleged abuse might have taken place. He stated to anyone who cared to listen (probably including the police) that if any such incident(s) had occurred he must have been drunk, because he certainly couldn't remember. The second oddity was that the wife did split with her husband at the time of the charges, but the pair of them got back together again later, and I think they're still married.

In physical terms there is little difference between the crime of incest and that of pedophilia, other than defining the criminal. There is a significant difference, however, in the terms of broken trust and continuing care, which perhaps explains why incest may be the charge rather than that of sexual assault of a child. There is also a significant difference in the habits of the criminal himself in instances where a father sexually assaults his daughter(s), even if over a period of time. There is a good chance that this is the only deviant crime he will ever commit, though of course that wasn't the case with my father. A side note: most available statistics on sibling incest reveal it to be significantly more common than parental incest, though far less seems to be heard about it.

The Mass Cover-up

If there is a single aspect of pedophilia that is beyond belief, it's the mass cover-up. In fact, in dwelling upon the guilt I felt for remaining silent for those twenty-plus years following Margaret's tearful story, the mass cover-up is the only condition that comes close to assuaging that guilt. It doesn't assuage it, of course. All it does is make me wonder about so many others who also "know" or "knew", and said nothing.

The most obvious cover-up on a grand scale is that done by the Catholic Church. Not so long ago, however, publicity focused hugely on Penn State and Sandusky, and whereas only one offender was involved at Penn, the media seems to place this crime on the same level as the Church. But then, that's America. The greater the scandal, etc. etc. There have been many other major cover-ups, of course. The Canadian residential school problem springs to mind, though most of the abuse there seems to have been physical and emotional.

Also of current interest is the Mormon polygamy sect in Bountiful, BC, that operated beyond the fringes of the law for so long, marrying off extremely young teenage girls to much older men. This abuse seems have been protected over a substantial period of time through the inaction of local authorities, despite circumstances that were well known to residents of the area, as well as the American police. It remained that way until someone finally took the case to the BC Supreme Court—and won. In March of 2012, the province finally gave the go-ahead to its prosecutors to lay polygamy charges, yet little seems to have been done to date about laying charges of sexual abuse for the alleged marriage of girls as young as twelve! And while this observation demonstrates a part of the problem with this crime, it also digresses from the topic.

The fairly recent examples in the news, the Catholic Church (there are new multi-case instances of abuse in Australia) and Penn State University, clearly demonstrate how intelligent, educated, and otherwise rational people will cover up a crime for causes so far not discussed. Their reasons move beyond the concerns of an abuse victim and his/her family, but the fundamental motivation remains the same.

On the surface, it would seem that the cover-up of the abuse was for the good of the large institution to which they belong, but which is, in the final analysis, their employer and source of livelihood. The people who try to hide the crimes are often very senior in the organization, and have been with the institution for many years. Over such a period of time, the institution has become the mainstay of their life. It is an integral part of their image and self-esteem. It has often become their *raison d'etre*.

In short, the institution, in many ways took on aspects of a second family. In fact, for those men and women who became employed by the Catholic Church, it probably becomes their family. As such, it doesn't take too much imagination to leap to the next stage. The institution and family to which they belong is being threatened, *ergo* it must be protected. This is the same kind of thinking often used by the mother of an abused child, and even the child itself, and all reason goes out the window. The wagons form a circle, and the cover-up begins. Only the real enemy, the pedophile, remains inside the circle of wagons, actually protected by the guns of those who know him for what he is. Meanwhile, outside the circle, the victims and the authorities become the enemy, seeking nothing more than justice.

Incredible, isn't it? So, idiotic as such suppression truly is, what are the motives behind such large-scale cover-ups that make intelligent people willing to break the law and abet a crime that has been perpetrated by someone whom they now probably despise anyway? I tried to make a list, in no particular order:

- A panicked reaction to a perceived threat to their pseudo family.
- The most foolish reason of all: the naive belief that the entire episode (which at first blush might seem to be localized, but is usually the tip of a huge iceberg) just might be covered up.
- The crime itself may reflect negatively on them as individuals for a variety of personal reasons: failure to do their job; fear that the fallout might rub off by association; concern about the reaction from or to their own family; negative press impact on self, family, and future.
- A possible loss of position or employment due to perceived neglect, public pressure, or the resulting negative impact on the institution itself.
- Protection of the institution's reputation.
- Protection of the institution's flow of funds.
- Protection of the principles on which the organization stands, and which have now been violated—even though it will be much worse if a cover-up is discovered.
- Possible protection of the individual involved because he's "not really a bad guy and he is a friend," though I suspect this isn't near the top of the list.
- Finally, plain stupidity. Reference the book already mentioned, *Why Smart People Do Dumb Things*, by Mortimer Feinberg, PhD.

When the word "family" is substituted for the word "institution," then the reasons for these huge cover-ups become a little more understandable, though no less deplorable. The end result is that a crime is being hidden (abetted), and for no valid reason: money and self-interest. And as always, the pedophile is assisted in continuing along his destructive path.

The above cover-ups that have been reported, along with huge amounts of money paid out in damages, clearly demonstrate the lack of common sense displayed by those who try to cover up such a crime. The moral corruption of self-interest on behalf of the hierarchies involved is instantly exposed, particularly that of the Catholic Church, an organization that by its very nature is supposed to set an example of the highest moral character. Yet the senior people involved appear blind to the fact that they are committing a crime by abetting it, which is astounding considering that they are, on the whole, fairly intelligent people. Paradoxically, none of them would aid and abet a mugger on the street, a crime that usually has far less impact on the victim.

The Catholic Church doesn't come any larger as an institution, nor is Penn State that small when compared to other universities (around 40,000 enrollment). Yet many men and some women, in collusion, hid and abetted pedophilia in an effort to ensure that the reputation and finances of their organization would not be harmed. Alas, this stance is probably fuelled by the fact that when the crime is discovered, the institution is liable for millions in legal claims by the victims. Ironically (darn, there's the word again), these cash suits may have played some part in finally bringing all this sexual abuse to light, and I must admit to mixed emotions on this topic.

One can grow quite cynical about the disproportionate number of people that seem to step forward where the sexual abusers have been in the employ of institutions with deep pockets. Monetary damage claims are now big business, one that seems to have played a large part in winkling out otherwise silent people, and convincing them to talk. To an extent, this has been a good thing. It can get out of hand, though. In several instances I've wondered whether a balance between culpability and redress has been maintained, particularly with offenders who are employees. With combined damage awards in the hundreds of millions, it's perhaps easy to understand why misguided officials run around attempting damage control, even if the act of doing so is both disgraceful and illegal.

As to the Catholic Church, they might try tackling something called prevention. Once the current debacle settles down, and time must surely see that take place, reducing the number of sexual abusers on the payroll is an area that needs to be vigorously addressed. A good start might be to touch up the Church recruiting policy by altering the rules to minimize sexual abuse and its subsequent cover-up. To an outsider, a good start in the right direction appears obvious. One of the key criteria for entering the Church and becoming (paradoxically) a "father" is celibacy.

The current policy of being celibate was introduced more than halfway through the Church's history, and was not strictly enforced until the late Middle Ages. It's no coincidence that this was the same era in which the Inquisition, flagellation and hair shirts were the rage, and a period during which the cruelty enforced by the Church's hierarchy was unmatched in religious history until today, with the surge in Muslim extremism.

The Vatican has abolished three of the above aberrations (the Inquisition, flagellation and hair shirts), but stubbornly clings to the ideal of denying its ordained staff the pleasure and/or release of sex desire through marriage (or, officially, any other means). This remains a key condition of employment, so perhaps as a minimum *mental* flagellation is still in vogue.

To distill the essence of this policy, once must look at the church's hiring process and its focus. Male employees are primarily recruited from young men whose hormones are flowing stronger than at any other time in their lives. They will never be hornier, and God/nature made them that way for a reason. (At that age I would have gladly said, "How about bringing back those hair shirts, and nixing the celibacy bit?") Yet the church is looking instead for these young men to say, "Yeah, okay, I understand. I'll give up sex and join you guys at the seminary."

Could this be setting the stage for a few problems later in life?

Ah, well, I suppose. The last few paragraphs might at first glance seem to wander off topic, but if a person is going to point out a problem, it doesn't hurt to suggest a solution.

On Progression

We want more and more and more, it is human nature. But this constant desire for "more" quickly becomes excess, and excess exists in many forms: greed; gluttony; murder; theft; drink; egoism; government spending and kids with candy (the last two are lumped together due to their similarity). All are the result of a progressive indulgence, and this applies to pedophilia, too. Had Margaret and I been privy to even one glimpse of almost any of today's web pages that profile pedophiles, we would have realized that the extent of Father's crimes was quite predictable. First, though, we would have had to figure out how to spell pedophile, then look it up to see what it meant. Finally, to be truly informed as to what to do about it, we would then have to sit pat for three decades waiting for our home computers, and another ten years for the Internet. Thank heavens that the information is now out there.

While nobody knows how far along Father's progression was when he abused me—just starting, or already ten years into it, for example—it clearly continued to expand afterward. Success breeds confidence, and confidence often has a habit of pushing aside common sense, which oddly enough can prove to be paradoxically fortuitous in a very tragic way. The more crimes a criminal commits, the more obvious they become, the more careless he gets, and the more inevitable it is that he will be caught.

I have seen this before. A white collar embezzler will steal maybe a few hundred dollars, often in a time of need, then sit back and do nothing more. Months later, when his need may actually be less, he recalls that he seems to have got away with the theft and so imagines the risk factor is less than he first believed. He steals again, and maybe a month and a half later does so once more—and once more. The amounts usually increase as well as the frequency, leaving a trail that now has many paw prints, rather than just the single one that might even have escaped detection. Bottom line: he will be caught.

Pedophiles are no different. By the time Father got to Steve, it turned out that the next door neighbour's daughter had also been abused, *whose parents also remained silent when they discovered this.* Did Mother know? She and the woman were very good friends, and remained so until into very old age. Of course she knew. There were undoubtedly others who also remained silent, either actual victims and/or their adult relatives. While the number will ever remain unknown, it was clear that Father's predatory behaviour became more frequent and much bolder as time went on.

In the following Appendix there are some statistics that stagger the mind. They certainly staggered mine, and added to the guilt over my ignorance. Victims of a single predator can number in the hundreds, and it makes me wonder just how far up the ladder of that statistic my father climbed.

There was one incident that so far I haven't related and, quite frankly, I never intended to. The incident seemed too vile and degrading to mention, for there is an illogical sense that the resulting shadow of shame clouds the whole family. But now, as I'm going through about the fifth draft of this manuscript, it's really dishonest to not relate the incident—especially in a section that deals with progression. It demonstrates how far matters had progressed beyond the realm of all the offences of which we imagined Father capable.

Margaret relayed the story as she was helping recall some of the details of her younger years. This happened years after the hearing when she was about fifty and father had already been sentenced. She was talking to an old friend at a party who had, it turned out, been abused by Father. This incident also demonstrated just how long abuse can remain silent and yet still boil up inside a victim's mind, before some event (father's trial) offers an opportunity to bring it out. The woman, whom both my sister and I have known since childhood, blurted that Father was the first male on whom she'd performed oral sex—at five or six years old. (Her comment was voiced in the vernacular, and was far more succinct.)

Shocking, isn't it? Working out all our ages, this incident would have taken place a couple of years after the abuse ended with me. It may have been just as it was ending with Margaret, or it could have been ongoing. Not that the timing matters. None of it should have happened!

By the time Father got to Steve, maybe as early as ten years after me, he had grown far bolder with the sexual abuse. His appetites were undoubtedly greater. They seemed to have broadened, both in range and in scope. In the meantime, two of his prior victims (Margaret and I), in our ignorance, were certain—or at least willing to believe—that he had reformed. Thus, by *not* telling anyone, we added to the confidence Father must have felt as he progressed (regressed) further and further down his destructive path.

Genetics

A brief comment on the possibility that pedophilia may be genetic. The idea has crossed my mind more than once, possibly motivated by nothing other than trepidation. I have looked up quite a few references and have rejected the notion based on what I found there, but this may have been done with the dark shade of bias. After all, my father was a pedophile. I sure as hell hope it's not genetic. Nonetheless, the topic both intrigued and concerned me at the same time. Nobody can deny that all living creatures have some form of genetic imprint that goes beyond the pure physical. Nature abounds with such empirical truths.

For example, take what happens with a cow and her newborn calf.

Until a few years ago, we opted to live on a farm and we raised cattle. When a cow gives birth, it's an event that is always exciting and awesomely amazing. This glistening, slippery wet being slithers from the womb and slides onto the ground. The cow is often standing, but if she's prone she'll heave herself to her feet and begin licking the calf dry, her huge raspy tongue serving as a rough stimulant for the calf's revivification. Within twenty minutes this small animal is tottering on shaky legs, and even before it gets its knobbly knees steady it's searching for food. It bumps against its mother, gets its bearing, and heads between her hind legs in search of milk. It noses around the mother's udder, butting and bunting until it finds a teat, then greedily begins to suck.

This is the most amazing part. And yes, it is instinct no doubt partly guided by the scent of the warm milk-laden udder, but even if it is, that still begs the question: how does it know this?

If you've never watched a calf stagger to life, then try to do so. You will be holding your breath, mentally trying to help the creature as it bangs its head up under its mother's belly trying to find that first drop of milk. The funny thing is, the speed and urge varies between each newly born critter, and some don't even have a clue. You have to hold the calf up to the spigot and stick a couple of fingers in its mouth as you squeeze milk from the teat with your free hand, teaching it how to drink. This raises another question: why do some know, and are incredibly aggressive; why do others, by comparison, seem to be helpless little waifs?

There have been many, many studies on the possibility that memory is passed down through genes. If they ever find that it is, it would certainly help explain so much of the seemingly ingrained hate in the world. The various experiments focus on learning curves as the benchmark, and the animal of choice is usually the long-suffering rat. As often happens with science when nothing is provable in terms of absolutes, such as blowing up an armoured tank with a new high explosive, opinion varies on the results. Scientists tracking rats, for example, might favour old theories when interpreting results, attributing such behaviour to instinct—which cannot be completely explained either. Yet surely instinct, too, is a genetic imprint that goes beyond the physical?

When it proves necessary to teach one small calf to drink while another eagerly bangs its head against mum's udder looking for milk, surely this shows that even instinct—or implanted memory—will vary in strength, perhaps in all living entities. Raising the stakes to a brain as large as the one inside a human skull, do similar and more complicated possibilities exist, including both the range and direction of the "instinctive" sexual urge?

There seems to be no definitive answer from the scientists. And as to the example of my father, there was another circumstance not mentioned so far, that perhaps should be. His brother, who remained in England, had two children. The oldest child was a boy, who led a lifestyle that makes a person speculate upon his family background (upbringing) and motivation. He remained reclusively single and lived in near hermit-like conditions, earning a living as a self-employed jewelry craftsman. His workshop was almost Dickensian, and he seemed to have little contact with the public. It was an unusual life, to say the least, and there is absolutely no evidence that he was sexually abused. Nevertheless, do elements of his lifestyle fit the profile? (Father's brother, by the way, was also self-employed, was equally ostentatious, and went bankrupt for the same silly reasons as my father.)

The youngest child was a girl, who was much more open and sociable than her brother. Being about the same age as Margaret, the two became friends during my sister's travels. Not long after Mother and Father's divorce, Marie and I were in England, and as usual visited her. She asked the reasons for the divorce, and I told her. From her reaction, which was not one of surprise, I believe she already had an inkling of the cause and wanted to talk. We both sat back and listened to what she had to say. It seems that her father had sexually abused her as well, though she offered no opinion regarding her brother. When she learned about my own 'male on male' experience, however, it seemed to open a new line of possibilities not previously explored. As so often happens, my cousin also thought she was alone—which she may or may not have been. But if not, and she and her brother followed the lead of their Canadian cousins, neither would have told the other what was happening anyway.

As to the genetics, well, oh boy. It would explain so much about the ingrained animosity and bias that seems to be embedded in so much of humanity. Nevertheless, when even scientists are unable to draw a conclusion about pedophilia and genetics, I opt for the line of thought they fall back on. It's one adopted by the medical community, specifically the psychiatrists. If a person is abused when young, sexually or otherwise, it significantly increases the odds that he or even she will become an abuser in turn. Since both my father and his brother fell into this category, the chance that they were also abused as children would be very high. That doesn't discount the possibility of a yet to be found genetic imprint, but I sincerely believe that the only reason I'm even talking about pedophilia is because I was sexually abused. In other words, being abused is what planted the topic in my mind to begin with. As such, there could well be a similar logic with those who are abused, and then abuse in turn: if it wasn't for their traumatic experiences as a child, such a notion would never have crossed their mind.

When I look at these last few lines, however, I realize that what I'm saying is that I really don't know for sure. I'm in good company. Nobody else seems to know, either.

Forgiveness

Several times over the years my brother Steve, ever the peacemaker, urged me to arrange a meeting with my father, though he bluntly said that the initiative would have to come from me. It seemed that Father had no particular interest in such a get-together. The reason was obvious, and Steve confirmed it. Since I was the only witness to testify, he held me responsible for his downfall. To phrase it another way, I had betrayed him. This meant that Father was the only member of the family still in denial, though by now this was almost certainly cognitive denial. This kind of attitude matches the profile of nearly all pedophiles as if it was an off-the-shelf template. Sandusky, despite the overwhelming evidence and his conviction, went to jail protesting his innocence, just as my father had done. And while it might seem odd that his wife also protested his innocence, could this also be a form of cognitive denial that assuages her own guilt in having been aware, but saying nothing?

When Steve called one day to ask if I wanted to meet up with Father, I told him there was no point in just getting together unless he at least said he wanted such a meeting, and my brother was good enough to say that had not happened. So I said, "Why bother?"

I suspect that Father had given a noncommittal hint that he would meet up if I wanted, which was probably why Steve later gave it another try. Father's stubborn streak was probably in play, and if Steve then told him that I really wanted to see him, which is the way things would have doubtless played out, he would then have "reluctantly" agreed. In this manner Father would have saved face.

Of course, there was the flip side to this. I suppose my stubborn streak was in play too, but to be brutally honest, I had no real urge to meet with my father—at the time. There really didn't seem to be any point in such a get-together. It could also have been that I just wasn't ready to confront old, dormant demons, particularly in the flesh. Or, another possible consideration: was I just being an S.O.B. as well?

I don't know how much time passed, but it wasn't long before Steve again raised the issue. Only this time it wasn't over a simple meeting, he suggested that I should tell Father that I forgave him for what had happened. It would make both of us feel better. Steve had probably already gone through the same process himself, though I never asked. My younger brother had always been soft at heart in such matters, possessing an endless need to mend family quarrels and get everyone speaking again, even if he had been active in the rift to begin with. Steve deserved credit for what he was trying to do, especially considering how Father, Mother, and then Oscar had treated him, and maybe there's a message there. But to forgive? What does that really mean?

By the time Steve once more phoned about a meeting, and the notion of forgiveness, I had given more thought to his suggestion. Not enough to change my mind perhaps, but enough to waver. The fact that Father didn't seem inclined to meet was the main reason for remaining negative. Even so, if feeling a bit uneasy about that decision means there was a bit of guilt, then I suppose I had a bit of guilt. This notion of forgiveness was a different concept from just a simple meeting, and I probably approached the idea with the accountant's cold, detached, rational methodology that is applied to most of his problems: I told Steve I'd think on it.

When I next spoke to him, the first thing I asked was if Father wanted to be forgiven. I half expected to hear him say yes, but instead he beat about the bush and finally said that Father probably hadn't really asked for any forgiveness at all. Steve then suggested, despite this, that forgiveness might be better all around just to clear the air, and maybe it might even make me feel better. I told him I was actually feeling quite fine thank you and asked if he was feeling fine too, and we both had a bit of chuckle. Father clearly figured he was in no need of forgiveness though, and my little brother was again just playing the peacemaker. Nonetheless, it made me think about forgiveness in general terms, what it meant and to whom, and it seemed to suddenly become clear—at least for me.

I told Steve that I couldn't see where it was possible to forgive in any true sense of the word, for Father's lack of any guilt or remorse seemed to make forgiveness moot. Forgiveness can only be given to somebody who regrets doing something wrong. Forgiveness is all about someone seeking solace and peace from the person he offended, which might in turn alleviate the guilt of his wrong. This simply wasn't the case here. Father never felt any regret about what he'd done, other than at being caught.

He hadn't asked to be forgiven, so the notion struck me as absurd. It would have been like emerging from an imagined emotional wilderness and saying, "Father, I forgive you." This conjured a double image of Father turning around after I'd spoken the words and staring at me. In one image, he simply looked baffled and said, "Huh?" In the other, he gives a smile of satisfaction that clearly said, "Gotcha."

As for the warm, fuzzy feeling of forgiveness that presumably washes over the forgiver, I suppose it works for some. I can't see the point of even mouthing the words, however, unless the recipient is at least sorry and regrets what he has done. Without that, a person might just as well address the sky and say, "Oh well, shit happens!" and get on with his life.

Oh, the things we say and do.

I found no comfort with that decision—not the forgiveness part, but in not meeting up with Father a few years before he died. In fact, I think another thin layer may have been added to the cold coating of guilt that already existed, due to those long years of silence. Steve maybe knew this without saying so, but such a meeting would have done no harm, and in the end I would at least have known more about my father in his declining years.

As mentioned before, he died in 2009, two months short of his ninety-second birthday. As my old Nan used say, as we sat around the living room fire in the same house in York where I was born, "It's a funny old world, isn't it Graham?"

APPENDIX

Definitions

Paraphilia: a pattern of recurring sexually arousing mental imagery or behaviour that involves unusual and especially socially unacceptable sexual practices (such as sadism or pedophilia). – *Merriam-Webster.com*. Merriam-Webster, 2012.

Pedophilia: (a form of paraphilia) a psychosexual disorder in which the fantasy or act of engaging in sexual activity with prepubescent children is the preferred or exclusive means of achieving sexual excitement and gratification. It may be homosexual or heterosexual. – *Mosbey's Medical Dictionary, 8th Edition*

Pedophile: a person who fantasizes about and is sexually aroused by prepubescent children (under the age of thirteen) for a period of six months. (Note: the definition simply uses the word "fantasizes." An individual does not have to act upon his/her fantasies in order to be classified as being a pedophile.) – Victims of Violence, Research Library: Pedophiles (http://www.victimsofviolence.on.ca/rev2/index.php)

Profile, Characteristics, and Behaviour Patterns of a Pedophile

Like so many other explanations found when I was researching certain parts of this book, the profile and characteristics of a pedophile seem to vary depending on the reference. As such, and also to demonstrate this oddity, I have drawn from two lists that do exactly that. The first is on the website of the Sheriff's

Office, Whatcom County, Bellingham, Washington (http://www.co.whatcom.wa.us/sheriff/sexoffenders/pedophile.jsp), as issued by The Department of Justice (US), and items are listed below as they appear. The second is from a list of characteristics used as a standard reference by many Canadian agencies such as the Canada Court Watch Program, and was initially prepared by Charles Montaldo (http://crime.about.com/od/sex/p/pedophile.htm). When dealing with the Montaldo summary, I list only the characteristics that differ from the list compiled by the US Department of Justice.

There seems to be basic agreement on the brief profile, however, so the Whatcom Country Sheriff's Office profile is used first, which is prefaced by the comment that the public in general has a misconception of just who the pedophile is likely to be.

US Department of Justice

Profile of a Pedophile

Child molesters come from all walks of life and from all socio-economic groups. They may be male or female, rich or poor, employed or unemployed, religious or non-religious, highly educated or uneducated, or from any race.

Characteristics and Behaviour Patterns of a Pedophile

1. Is most often an adult male.
2. Is usually married.
3. Works in a wide range of occupations, from unskilled labourer to corporate executive.
4. Relates better to children than adults.
5. Socializes with few adults unless they are pedophiles.
6. Usually prefers children in a specific age group.
7. Usually prefers either males only or females only, but may be bisexual.
8. May seek employment or volunteer with programs involving children of the age of his preference.

9. Pursues children for sexual purposes.
10. Frequently photographs or collects photographs of his victims, either dressed, nude, or in sexually explicit acts.
11. Collects child erotica and child-adult pornography.
12. May possess and furnish narcotics to his victims to lower their inhibitions.
13. Is usually intelligent enough to recognize that he has a personal problem and understands the severity of it.
14. May go to great lengths to conceal his illegal activity.
15. Often rationalizes his illicit activities, emphasizing his positive impact upon the victim and repressing feelings about the harm that he has done.
16. Often portrays the child as the aggressor. This usually occurs after the child realizes that by withholding "sexual favours" the child will obtain what he or she desires, such as new toys, clothing or trips.
17. Talks about children in the same manner as one would talk about an adult lover or spouse.
18. Often was a child molestation victim and frequently seeks out children at the age or stage of physical development at which he was molested.
19. Often seeks out publications and organizations that support his sexual beliefs and practices.
20. Usually corresponds with other pedophiles and exchanges child pornography and erotica as proof of involvement.
21. Is usually non-violent and has few problems with the law (pedophiles are frequently respected community members).

This list is followed by further information that begins with the following:

The widespread misconception *that child molestation consists solely of children being seized from the street and forcibly molested couldn't be further from the truth. Although these incidents do occur,* the vast majority of child molesters are adults who seduce children through subtle intimidation and persuasion and are known to the child.

Differences/Additions Found in the Montaldo List

1. Often is male and over thirty years of age.
2. Often is single or with few friends in his age group.
3. If he's married, the relationship is more "companion" based, with no sexual relations.
4. He is often vague about time gaps in employment, which may indicate loss of employment for questionable reasons or possible past incarceration.
5. He will often refer to children in pure or angelic terms, using descriptions like innocent, heavenly, divine, pure, and other words that describe children but seem inappropriate and exaggerated.
6. He has hobbies that are childlike, such as collecting popular expensive toys, keeping reptiles or exotic pets, or building planes or car models.

Note: The characteristics, quite appropriately, come with a caution that the (complete) list is merely an indicator and it should not be assumed that individuals with such characteristics are actually pedophiles.

Statistics

Both in Canada and the US, it is difficult to find statistics that are current (five years old or less). Most that are available, even on government websites, seem to add another ten years to that figure. As such, many of the statistics garnered are over ten years old, but likely haven't changed significantly. Those immediately following are drawn from the website of an organization called Yello Dyno (http://www.yellodyno.com/html/child_molester_stats.html), whose title page includes the words *Protecting Children from Child Predators*. This is a US-based, non-profit organization with the primary goal of preventing child victimization. While the statistics are also US figures, they come from a much larger base, which should remove more of the "bumps." Each statistic is annotated on the organization's site.

1. There are more than 400,000 *registered* sex offenders in the US, and an estimated 80,000 to 100,000 of them are missing (Based on population, Canada's statistics would run about 10% of these figures.). Their addresses are supposed to be registered, but the authorities no longer know where they are.
2. Between 1% and 5% of the population molests children.
3. Males committed 96% of the sexual assaults on children that were reported to law enforcement.
4. Offenders under eighteen committed 23% of sexual assaults on children; 77% were committed by adults.
5. Sexual assaults against the very young are rarely by strangers; they (strangers) account for only 3% of victims under six, and account for 5% of victims between six and eleven.
6. Of child victimizers in State prisons one third committed the crime against their own children, and around (a further) one half had a relationship with the victim as a friend, relative or acquaintance.
7. Taking all ages into account, approximately 90% of offenders are known to the child victim. In total, the offenders are 29% relatives; 60% acquaintances; and 11% strangers.
8. Of the *violent* victimizations of children, 75% took place in either the victim's home or that of the offender.
9. In general, 43% of all child assaults took place in the victim's home; 42% took place in the offender's home.
10. The typical pedophile/molester is male, begins molesting by age fifteen, and molests an average of 117 youngsters.

11. 75% of sexual abuse victims are abused more than once.
12. 70% to75% of offenders are under the age of thirty-five.
13. Though not officially categorized as sexual abuse, the highest incidence of incest takes place among siblings (this crime is tallied as incest even where children are involved, not sexual assault).
14. Three in ten victimizers (offenders) against children were reported as having multiple victims.
15. Like rape, child molestation is one of the most unreported crimes, of which probably no more than an estimated 10% are reported.
16. Of all sexual assaults handled by law enforcement agencies (US Department of Justice), 67% of victims were below the age of majority. One in seven was under the age of six, and over a third were under the age of twelve.
17. Around 75% of child sexual abuse victims are girls.
18. The rate of sexual abuse among children with disabilities is 1.75 times higher than that among children without disabilities.
19. Children between the ages of twelve and seventeen are beaten, raped, and robbed five times more often than adults.
20. Children aged twelve and up, particularly teens, account for the vast majority of actual long-term child abductions (and murders); the numbers are dramatically higher among the fourteen- to seventeen-year-olds.
21. Research has shown that the absence of a parent from the home increases the child's risk. This fits, at least in part, with the perpetrator's preferred profile of his victim: young, isolated, depressed, or lonely.

22. More than 2,900,000 incidents of child abuse in some form (sexual, physical, neglect, etc.) were reported in 2003, which represented approximately 1% of the entire US population.

A few more statistics for Canada, taken from Juristat (http://www.statcan.gc.ca/pub/85-002-x/index-eng.htm), the Canadian Centre for Justice Statistics, as put out by Statistics Canada:

1. In 1997, there were 30,735 sex offences of all kinds reported to the police, representing 10% of all violent crimes.
2. New, firmer legislation on sexual assault was passed in 1983, and the rate of reported sex offences rose dramatically until 1993, peaking at 135 incidents per 100,000 population. This subsequently dropped by 25%, but levelled out at 74% higher than before the legislation was passed. Since estimated unreported sex offences might run as high as 90%, the new law helped, but not so much as to be highly successful.
3. In 1997, males accounted for 85% of all violent offences, but 98% of all sexual offences. The respective median ages were twenty-nine and thirty-two.
4. In 1997–1998, 57% of sex offenders were sentenced to prison in adult provincial/territorial facilities (compared to federal), compared to 38% of violent offenders. Prison terms for sex offenders were longer, with 37% exceeding one year, compared to 14% for violent offenders.
5. Of all inmates registered in Canadian jails on October 5, 1996, 9% were sex offenders. They accounted for 7% of inmates serving less than two years; 14% of those serving two or more years.
6. Almost half of federal inmates over fifty-five were sex offenders.

7. In 1997, data indicated that 62% of all sex offence victims were under eighteen; 24% of the victims of violent offences were under eighteen. 82% of all sex offence victims were female; 18% were male. However, for victims under twelve, this changed to 69% female and 31% male.
8. And finally, a detail from an online Canadian Department of Justice site that gives estimates of the annual public cost of child abuse for 2004, as assembled using the Day model. The cost categories are broken into the categories of Social Services, Employment, Judicial, Personal, and several lesser classifications, and amount to just under sixteen billion dollars. That cost would doubtless be significantly greater today.

To order more copies of this book, find books by other
Canadian authors, or make inquiries about publishing your own
book, contact PageMaster at:

PageMaster Publication Services Inc.
11340-120 Street, Edmonton, AB T5G 0W5
books@pagemaster.ca
780-425-9303

catalogue and e-commerce store
www.ShopPageMaster.ca

About the Author

Graham Clews is a retired chartered accountant who lives in Westlock, Alberta. *The Sound of Silence* is his fifth book, though the last of his seven books to be published. Other writing includes *Jessica Jones and The Gates of Penseron*, a young adult fantasy novel with a unique approach to time travel; a Roman/Celtic saga, *The Eboracum Trilogy*, that follows three generations through the founding of York in the first century; *Politically Detained*, a rogue minister of finance and a half dozen irate seniors skirt the law attempting to reform parliament; and *A Slightly Tainted Hero*, a panicked, sixty year old accountant successfully tackles an armed mugger, only to find past sins emerge as his instant fame goes viral. Graham has also won recognition over the years for his poetry.

Full details and a more detailed biography can be found on his website: www.graham-clews.com